D0782985

Swift 4 Recipes

Hundreds of Useful Hand-picked Code Snippets

Yanis Zafirópulos

Apress®

Swift 4 Recipes: Hundreds of Useful Hand-picked Code Snippets

Yanis Zafirópulos
Granada, Spain

ISBN-13 (pbk): 978-1-4842-4181-3   ISBN-13 (electronic): 978-1-4842-4182-0
https://doi.org/10.1007/978-1-4842-4182-0

Library of Congress Control Number: 2018963844

Copyright © 2019 by Yanis Zafirópulos

This work is subject to copyright. All rights are reserved by the Publisher, whether the whole or part of the material is concerned, specifically the rights of translation, reprinting, reuse of illustrations, recitation, broadcasting, reproduction on microfilms or in any other physical way, and transmission or information storage and retrieval, electronic adaptation, computer software, or by similar or dissimilar methodology now known or hereafter developed.

Trademarked names, logos, and images may appear in this book. Rather than use a trademark symbol with every occurrence of a trademarked name, logo, or image we use the names, logos, and images only in an editorial fashion and to the benefit of the trademark owner, with no intention of infringement of the trademark.

The use in this publication of trade names, trademarks, service marks, and similar terms, even if they are not identified as such, is not to be taken as an expression of opinion as to whether or not they are subject to proprietary rights.

While the advice and information in this book are believed to be true and accurate at the date of publication, neither the authors nor the editors nor the publisher can accept any legal responsibility for any errors or omissions that may be made. The publisher makes no warranty, express or implied, with respect to the material contained herein.

Managing Director, Apress Media LLC: Welmoed Spahr
Acquisitions Editor: Aaron Black
Development Editor: James Markham
Coordinating Editor: Jessica Vakili

Cover image designed by Freepik (www.freepik.com)

Distributed to the book trade worldwide by Springer Science+Business Media New York, 233 Spring Street, 6th Floor, New York, NY 10013. Phone 1-800-SPRINGER, fax (201) 348-4505, e-mail orders-ny@springer-sbm.com, or visit www.springeronline.com. Apress Media, LLC is a California LLC and the sole member (owner) is Springer Science + Business Media Finance Inc (SSBM Finance Inc). SSBM Finance Inc is a Delaware corporation.

For information on translations, please e-mail rights@apress.com, or visit http://www.apress.com/rights-permissions.

Apress titles may be purchased in bulk for academic, corporate, or promotional use. eBook versions and licenses are also available for most titles. For more information, reference our Print and eBook Bulk Sales web page at http://www.apress.com/bulk-sales.

Any source code or other supplementary material referenced by the author in this book is available to readers on GitHub via the book's product page, located at www.apress.com/978-1-4842-4181-3. For more detailed information, please visit http://www.apress.com/source-code.

Printed on acid-free paper

To my father
For having introduced me to the world of
programming, 25 years ago; and with the hope
that he will finally get himself a Mac.

Table of Contents

About the Author

Yanis Zafirópulos is a Spain-based programmer and Mac convert, who adores any coding challenge and has been in love with the Art of Coding since he was a little kid. In his former life, he pretended to become a doctor, but – for everyone's sake – this never happened. In this one, he pretends he is still a Computer Science undergraduate student.

In his free time, he likes writing, reading, drawing, collecting, cycling, linguistics, playing chess, creating programming languages, and pretty much anything that catches his eye.

He's also the main developer and editor of the iSwift website, featuring an Objective-C to Swift converter – with the same name – as well as a vast collection of Swift-related tools and resources.

So, if you're interested, feel free to check this out too: `https://iswift.org`

About the Technical Reviewer

Felipe Laso is a Senior Systems Engineer working at Lextech Global Services. He's also an aspiring game designer/programmer. You can follow him on Twitter as @iFeliLM or on his blog.

Acknowledgments

I would like to thank Aaron, Jessica, Jim, Felipe (thank you so much!) and the whole Apress team for helping me make this book a reality.

And of course, all the legends: Bill, Steve, Linus, Andrew, Edsger, Richard, Niklaus, Rasmus, Chris, Matz, Guido, Dennis, Bjarne... without whose inspiration, the author of this book might never have become a programmer.

PART I

Beginner

CHAPTER 1

Introduction

Now that you have gotten your hands on this little book, let's get them a bit... dirty. And what's better than delving into our first program?

In this chapter, we'll see how we can write our first program in Swift, compile it, run it, and even see how Swift can be used as a scripting language.

1-1. Getting Familiar with Swift

Problem

You'd like to execute and compile a simple Swift program that you just created.

Solution

Fire up your favorite editor, and let's write this very basic one line of code.

```
print("Hello Swift!")
```

How It Works

Now that we already have our code file, let's save this as `hello.swift`. The next rather logical question is: *How do we actually run this thing?*

© Yanis Zafirópulos 2019
Y. Zafirópulos, *Swift 4 Recipes*, https://doi.org/10.1007/978-1-4842-4182-0_1

Executing It

Well, you might be expecting something along the lines of "Open Xcode, etc, etc," but - since I'm rather old-school and prefer having total control over what goes on, why/how it is executed, and so on - what could be better than doing it straight from the command line?

So, just open the Terminal app and let's go to the location where your `hello.swift` resides. Now, all that's left – provided that you already have Xcode installed (and the accompanying developer tools) – is running our script:

```
swift hello.swift
```

And here is the output:

```
Hello Swift!
```

That was easy, wasn't it? Pretty much like with any scripting language (see PHP, Python, Ruby, Perl, etc.). But wait: Is Swift a scripting language? Well, not quite...

Compiling It

What if we actually want to compile this code of ours and have a binary, which we can then use, without having to recompile or keep the Swift compiler around?

Let's see...

```
swiftc hello.swift
```

Super easy again, nope? Just note the use of `swiftc` (the Swift compiler) instead of `swift`.

Now, if you look again into your folder contents, you'll notice a single `hello` binary, which you can execute, like any normal binary:

```
./hello
```

And that was it.

1-2. Scripting in Swift

Problem

You'd like to use Swift for Scripting, pretty much like any regular interpreted language, such as PHP, Python, Ruby, Perl, or... even Bash.

Well, here's the catch: given its speed, it sure can: at least for smaller scripts. Plus, since Apple has already launched it as open source software (already having been ported to Linux), this makes it a not-so Mac-only thing.

So, the answer is: *Why not?*

Solution

Start with the same **Hello World** script we played with in the previous section.

But now, let's add the magic *shebang* line: `#!/usr/bin/env swift`

What we do here with this magic initial line is to help our Terminal recognize our script as executable source code – otherwise, it'll be treated as some random text: we basically tell Bash which compiler to use (Swift), and actually to look for it (`/usr/bin/env`).

```
#!/usr/bin/env swift
print("Hello Swift!")
```

We save it as `hello_script.swift`. And that was it.

How It Works

First, we make it "officially" executable by:

```
sudo chmod +x hello_script.swift
```

5

We can now execute it as we would execute any script:

```
./hello_script.swift
```

Yay! Now, it's time to rock'n'roll! :)

1-3. Summary

In this chapter, we've seen how you can get started with Swift easily so that you're able to write and execute your application.

In the next section, now that you have all the basic tools set up, we'll begin digging into the basics of the Swift language and step-by-step explore all of the techniques that'll turn you into a top-notch Swift programmer.

CHAPTER 2

Basics

In this chapter, we will look into some basic constructs and conventions of the Swift programming language and help you get started writing your first program.

2-1. Create a Hello World

Problem

I want to write a Hello World program and write my first Swift program.

Solution

A single line does the trick. Hello World!

```
print("Hello World!")
```

How It Works

All we have to write is a single line of code, using the print function.

```
Hello World!
```

2-2. Declare variables

Problem

We want to declare some variables.

Solution

Declare a variable, without type.

```
var surname = "Doe"
```

Declare a variable, with type.

```
var fullName : String = "John Doe"
```

And another one ...

```
var age : Int = 25
```

Now, since it's a variable, why not change it?

```
age = 32
```

So, let's see what we've done.

```
print("My name is \(surname). \(fullName). And I'm \(age) years old.")
```

How It Works

Variables are at the very core of every program. Basically, they consist of an identifier (symbolic name) associated with a value, which - in contrast with constants - can change.

```
My name is Doe. John Doe. And I'm 32 years old.
```

2-3. Declare constants
Problem

We want to declare some constants.

Solution

Declare a constant, without type.

```
let surname = "Doe"
```

Declare a constant, with type.

```
let fullName : String = "John Doe"
```

And another one.

```
let age : Int = 32
```

If we attempt to reassign any of the above, like: `age = 31`
the compiler will complain. So, just don't do it.
If you want to be able to change them, just use variables, not constants.
So, let's see what we've done...

```
print("My name is \(surname). \(fullName). And I'm \(age) years old.")
```

How It works

A **Constant** is a value that - in contrast to variables - cannot be altered by the program during normal execution.

```
My name is Doe. John Doe. And I'm 32 years old.
```

2-4. Declare multiple variables

Problem

I want to declare multiple variables.

Solution

```
var red, green, blue : Double
```

or even assign all of them on the same line:

```
var name = "John", surname = "Doe"
```

So... what's my name?

```
print("My name is \(name) \(surname)! Not really…")
```

How It Works

You can declare *multiple* variables of the same type, in the same line.

```
My name is John Doe! Not really...
```

2-5. Declare Unicode constants and variables

Problem

AI want to declare constants and variables with Unicode names.

Solution

So, setting a constant this way is absolutely correct Swift code

```
let π = 3.14159
```

Or, even this one - now, let's set a variable.

```
var 好好 = "ni hao"
```

Let's use our variable.

```
print("'Hello' in Mandarin Chinese = \(好好)")
```

How It Works

In Swift, constant and variable names can contain *almost* any character, including Unicode characters.

```
'Hello' in Mandarin Chinese = ni hao
```

2-6. Declare a range
Problem

I want to declare a range.

Solution

Let's declare a range constant
which will include numbers from 0 up to 4, including 4
meaning: 0, 1, 2, 3, 4
    This is called a "closed" range

We'll be using the ... operator

```
let closedRange = 0...4
```

Now let's declare another "open" range constant (or a half-open one, to be precise)
which will include numbers from 0 up to 4, but not including 4
meaning: 0, 1, 2, 3

We'll be using the ..< operator

```
let openRange = 0..<4
```

Time to greet ourselves now!

```
for _ in openRange {
    print("Hello mate!")
}
```

How It Works

Declaring a **Range** is very practical (especially in loops). And easy as well. All you have to do use the ellipse symbol (...) - to declare closed ranges - or its variation (..<), to declare open ranges.

```
Hello mate!
Hello mate!
Hello mate!
Hello mate!
```

2-7. Define an enumeration type

Problem

I want to define an Enumeration.

Solution

So, let's define a new enumeration - a number will either be even, or odd

```
enum Divisible {
    case even
    case odd
}
```

First, we create a Divisible variable and initialize it.

```
var div = Divisible.even
```

Let's sec...

```
print("Number is \(div)")
```

Now, let's change its value

Tip   Now that the compiler knows the variable's type, that's it's a Divisible enumeration, we can also use the shorthand notation. That is: `.even` or `.odd` - instead of `Divisible.even` and `Divisible.odd`

```
div = .odd
```

Let's check it again.

```
print("Number is now \(div)")
```

How It Works

An **Enumeration** defines a common type for a group of related values and enables you to work with those values in a *type-safe* way within your code. In Swift, this can be easily done by using the enum keyword.

```
Number is even
Number is now odd
```

2-8. Define a type alias

Problem

I want to define a type alias.

Solution

Let's say how we call strings.

```
typealias CharacterArray = String
```

OK, a string is practically an array of characters. Sounds legit.
Let's use our new type alias now

```
let str : CharacterArray = "Hello World!"
```

And let's see it printed.

```
print(str)
```

How It Works

A **Type Alias** declares an alternative name for an existing type. In swift, in order to define a new type alias, you may use the keyword `typealias`.

```
Hello World!
```

2-9. Use semicolons

Problem

I want to be able to use semicolons.

Solution

So, do you have to use semicolons?

```swift
var nope = "no, you don't" // well, mostly
```

You may use them whenever you wish and the compiler won't complain.

```swift
var a = 2; // just like that
```

However, you have to use them if you want to write more than one single statements on the same line.

Like this:

```swift
let greeting = "Hello World!"; print(greeting)
```

How It Works

Generally, unlike many other languages, Swift does not require you to write a semicolon (;) after each statement in your code, although you can do so if you wish. A notable exception is when you have more than one single statements in the same line.

```swift
Hello World!
```

2-10. Use comments
Problem

I want to be able to use comments in my code.

Solution

Comments may be single-line. Like this one.

```
// Beginning with 2 forward slashes

/* Or even multi-line, starting with a forward-slash followed
by an asterisk
    and ending with an asterisk followed by a forward-slash.

    Yep, just like that. */

/* We can "nest" them, too.
    /* Meaning: too include a comment, within a comment. */
    This sounds rather Inception-ish, I must say.
*/
```

How It Works

Comments can be found in practically any - reasonable - program and are the easiest way to either annotate your source code or even debug it (by *commenting-out* code). Commenting out code can be done either by using // to comment-out a single line of code, or by using /* .. */ to comment-out entire sections, possibly covering multiple lines of code.

2-11. Summary

In this chapter, we've seen how you can get started with Swift: from writing our very first program, to declaring variables, constants, or being able to use some basic concepts, like comments in our code.

In the next chapter, get ready for something more advanced: we'll begin looking into the use of Conditional statements in Swift.

CHAPTER 3

Conditionals

Conditionals are at the very core of every programming language. A conditional statement allows us to perform different computations or actions depending on whether a specific Boolean condition evaluates to `true` or `false`, thus making changing program flow possible.

3-1. Write an if statement

Problem

I want to write a simple `if` statement.

Solution

```
var sunnyWeather = true

if sunnyWeather {
    print("Sure it's sunny. Let's go for a walk!")
}
```

How It Works

In its simplest form, the **if statement** has a single if condition. In a nutshell: it executes its block of statements only if that condition is *true*.

```
Sure it's sunny. Let's go for a walk!
```

3-2. Write an if/else statement

Problem

I want to write a simple if / else statement.

Solution

```
var sunnyWeather = false

if sunnyWeather {
    print("Sure it's sunny. Let's go for a walk!")
} else {
    print("Awesome. Let's stay at home and write some
Swift!")
}
```

How It Works

An **if statement** can also provide alternative statements in case its initial condition is not true. This is where *if-else* statements come into play.

```
Awesome. Let's stay at home and write some Swift!
```

3-3. Write multiple if/else/if statements

Problem

I want to write multiple if, or if / else statements.

Solution

Let's set our control variable.

```
var temperature = 30 // Not that cold; it's in Celsius, guys

if temperature < 10 {
    print("Hmm, that's pretty fresh...")
} else if temperature >= 10 && temperature < 30 {
    print("Nice temperature!")
} else {
    print("Hmm, it's getting rather hot...")
}
```

How It Works

If a single if/else statement is not enough, you can chain as many else if statements as you wish.

```
Hmm, it's getting rather hot...
```

3-4. Write a switch statement
Problem

I want to write a switch statement.

Solution

Let's set our control variable.

```
let vehicle = "Bicycle"
```

What type of vehicle is it? Let's see...

```
switch vehicle {

    case "Car":
         print("You have 4 wheels. Nice!")
    case "Bicycle":
         print("You have 2 wheels. Yay!")

    // what happens if it's none of the above? Hmm...

    default:
         print("I have no idea how many wheels you've got.")
         print("But, you're still awesome! ;-)")
}
```

How It Works

A **Switch statement** is a great way to check an expression against different values, without having to chain endless if-else ifs. In Swift, this can be done by using the switch construct, while designating the different cases by using the case keyword.

```
You have 2 wheels. Yay!
```

3-5. Write a switch statement with intervals

Problem

I want to write a switch statement, but using intervals – instead of values – for the different cases.

Solution

Let's set our control variable.

```
var temperature = 30 // Not that cold; it's in Celsius, guys

switch temperature {

    case -20..<0:
        print("Icy cold! Brrr...")
    case 0..<10:
        print("That's rather fresh")
    case 10..<25:
        print("Nice temperature!")
    case 25..<35:
        print("Getting hotter...")

    // what happens if it's none of the above? Hmm...
    // Basically when temperature >= 35

    default:
        print("Oops! That's hot!")
}
```

How It Works

A **Switch statement** is a great way to check an expression against different values. But you can also check against different intervals/ranges. Sounds perfect, right?

In Swift, this can be done by using ranges instead of specific values.

```
Getting hotter...
```

3-6. Write a switch statement with enumeration values

Problem

I want to write a switch statement, making use of enumerations.

Solution

Let's quickly define an enumeration type.

```
enum Direction {
    case north
    case east
    case south
    case west
}
```

Let's set our control variable.

```
let dir = Direction.south
```

What type of vehicle is it? Let's see...

```
switch dir {

    case .north:
        print("Heading north. Nice!")
    case .east:
        print("Heading east. Great!")
    case .south:
        print("Fly down south, hide your head in the sand...")
    case .west:
        print("The west is the best...")

}
```

How It Works

A **Switch statement** is a great way to check an expression against different values. And an **enumeration** is a great of grouping relevant values together.

```
Fly down south, hide your head in the sand...
```

3-7. Write a switch statement with compound cases

Problem

I want to write a `switch` statement with multiple values for each case.

Solution

Let's set our control variable.

```
var letter = "j"
switch letter {
    case "a", "e", "i", "o", "u":
    print("It's a vowel.")

    case "b", "c", "d", "f", "g", "h", "j", "k", "l", "m", "n",
     "p", "q", "r", "s", "t", "v", "w", "x", "y", "z":
    print("It's a consonant.")

    default:
    print("It's neither a vowel, nor a consonant - what could
    it be?!")

}
```

How It Works

Switch statements are very flexible: we can also stack more than one value/ match that are under the same case and share the same statement body.

```
It's a consonant.
```

3-8. Write a switch statement with tuples

Problem

I want to write a switch statement, using tuples for each case.

Solution

Let's set our control variable.

```
var temperature = ("Celsius", 30) // Not that cold; it's in
Celsius, guys

switch temperature {
    case ("Celsius", 0):
        print("Perfect zero - in Celsius")
    case ("Fahrenheit", 0):
        print("Perfect zero - in Fahrenheit")

    // to match anything - either Celsius or Fahrenheit - use '_'
    case (_, -20..<0):
        print("Either in Celsius, or in Fahrenheit, that's
        coooold!")

    // what happens if it's none of the above? Hmm...
    // No, I'm not going to cover every possible temperature
    range
```

```
default:
        print("None of the above matched. Oh well...")
```

}

How It Works

A **Switch statement** is a great to check an expression against different values. But, using **tuples**, you can also check against two (or more) different values at the same time. Not bad, huh?

```
None of the above matched. Oh well...
```

3-9. Write a switch statement with value bindings

Problem

I want to write a switch statement, while also catching the different matched values.

Solution

Let's set our control variable.

```
var temperature = ("Celsius", 0)
```

```
switch temperature {
    // match against any first value
    // and store it in the variable 'system'
    case (let system, 0):
        print("Perfect zero - in \(system)")
```

25

```
    // what happens if it's none of the above? Hmm...
    // This time we can omit 'default' and just store the tuple

case let (system, degrees):
        print("None of the above matched. Temperature is \
        (degrees) degrees - in \(system).")

}
```

How It Works

A **Switch statement** is a powerful construct. But, using **tuples** with value
bindings, you can also check against two (or more) different values at
the same time and bind the value/s it matches to temporary constants or
variables, which can be used in the body of the case. Awesome.

```
Perfect zero - in Celsius
```

3-10. Use the ternary conditional operator
Problem

I want to use the ternary conditional operator - ?.

Solution

Let's set our control variable.

```
var sunnyWeather = false

// It works like this:
// condition ? do-something : do-something-else

sunnyWeather ? print("Yeah, it's sunny") : print("Too bad...")
```

```
// Or we can embed it inside another statement
// Does the exact same thing as the above statement

print(sunnyWeather ? "Yeah, it's sunny" : "Too bad...")
```

How It Works

The **ternary operator** (?) is the shorthand of a basic *if-else* statement. And it looks rather neat, too.

```
Too bad...
Too bad...
```

3-11. Use the nil coalescing operator

Problem

I want to use the nil coalescing operator - ??.

Solution

Basically, it's the equivalent of: a != nil ? a! : b.

Or: if a is not nil, unwrap it. Otherwise: return b.

Let's set our control variables.

```
let systemBackgroundSetting = "blue"
var userBackgroundSetting : String? // This is an optional, and
it automatically set to nil
```

Has the user played with the Settings?

If not, return the default system setting...

```
var currentBackground = userBackgroundSetting ??
systemBackgroundSetting

print("Current background color: \(currentBackground)")
```

How It Works

The **nil coalescing operator** (??) is used to either unwrap an optional variable, or - if it's nil - return an alternative value.

```
Current background color: blue
```

3-12. Use the logical and operator

Problem

I want to use the logical and operator.

Solution

Let's define some test Boolean variables.

```
let weatherIsSunny = true
let notRaining = true
```

Now, let's try it out in an if statement...

```
if weatherIsSunny && notRaining {
    print("Weather is great. Let's go for a walk!")
} else {
    print("Hmm... maybe stay at home?")
}
```

How It Works

The **logical and** operator (&&) is used to combine two *Boolean* expressions. The final expression is true, only if both of the initial expressions are true.

```
Weather is great. Let's go for a walk!
```

3-13. Use the logical not operator

Problem

I want to use the logical not operator.

Solution

Let's define some test Boolean variables.

```
let weatherIsSunny = false
```

Now, let's try it out in an if statement...

```
if !weatherIsSunny {
    print("It's not sunny. It might be raining...")
} else {
    print("Yep, it's sunny")
}
```

How It Works

The **logical not** operator (!) is used to negate/invert a *Boolean* expression. The final expression is true, only if the initial expression is false.

```
It's not sunny. It might be raining...
```

3-14. Use the logical or operator

Problem

I want to use the logical or operator.

Solution

Let's define some test Boolean variables.

```
let weatherIsSunny = true
let notRaining = true
```

   Now, let's try it out in an if statement...

```
if weatherIsSunny || notRaining {
    print("Weather is fine. Let's go for a walk!")
} else {
    print("Hmm... maybe stay at home?")
}
```

How It Works

The **logical or** operator (||) is used to combine two *Boolean* expressions. The final expression is true if any one of the initial expressions is true.

```
Weather is fine. Let's go for a walk!
```

3-15. Use the logical xor operator

Problem

I want to use the logical xor operator.

Solution

Although there is no predefined XOR operator - as with OR/AND/NOT - we can use the following concept:

```
A XOR B => A != B
```

So, let's define some test Boolean variables.

```
let hamburgers = true
let pizza = false
```

Now, let's try it out in an if statement...

```
if hamburgers != pizza {
    print("Nice! Time to eat!")
} else {
    print("Hmm... you have to finally make up your mind!")
}
```

How It Works

The **logical xor** operator - or the "exclusive or" - is used to combine two *Boolean* expressions. The final expression is true, if only one - but not both - of the initial expressions is true.

```
Nice! Time to eat!
```

3-16. Summary

In this chapter, we've seen how you can use conditional statements in Swift: from simple if or if/else statements, to using more complex switch constructs, and even using the logical operators (and, or, not, xor).

In the next chapter, we'll see how we can give our program even more flexibility by making use of the power of loops.

CHAPTER 4

Loops

In computer programming, a loop is a control flow statement for specifying iteration, which allows code to be executed repeatedly. In this chapter, we'll look into the different ways that you can use them in Swift.

4-1. Write a for loop

Problem

I want to write a for loop.

Solution

Let's write a simple loop.

```
for x in 0...5 {
    print("x = \(x)")
}
```

If you don't need the current value from the sequence, then you can just ignore it by replacing the variable name with an underscore.

```
for _ in 0..<3 {
    print("Hello world!")
}
```

© Yanis Zafirópulos 2019
Y. Zafirópulos, *Swift 4 Recipes*, https://doi.org/10.1007/978-1-4842-4182-0_4

How It Works

You may use a **for-in loop** to iterate over a sequence, for example, a range of numbers, items in an array, characters in a string, etc.

```
x = 0
x = 1
x = 2
x = 3
x = 4
x = 5
Hello world!
Hello world!
Hello world!
```

4-2. Write a while loop
Problem

I want to write a While loop.

Solution

Set an initial value for our control variable.

```
var x = 0
```

Let's loop!

```
while x<10 {
     print("x = \(x)")
     x += 1
}
```

x<10 is not true anymore (x became 10), so here we are...

```
print("Finished.")
```

How It Works

A **While loop** is a loop that - in contrast with a *Repeat-While* one - evaluates its condition at the start of each pass.

```
x = 0
x = 1
x = 2
x = 3
x = 4
x = 5
x = 6
x = 7
x = 8
x = 9
Finished.
```

4-3. Write a repeat-while loop
Problem

I want to write a Repeat-While loop.

Solution

Set an initial value for our control variable.

```
var x = 0
```

Let's loop!

```
repeat {
    print("x = \(x)")
    x += 1
} while x<10
```

x<10 is not true anymore (x became 10), so here we are...

```
print("Finished.")
```

How It Works

A **Repeat-While** loop is a loop that - in contrast to a *While loop* - evaluates its condition at the end of each pass.

```
x = 0
x = 1
x = 2
x = 3
x = 4
x = 5
x = 6
x = 7
x = 8
x = 9
Finished.
```

4-4. Summary

In this chapter, we've seen how to make use of the power of loops in Swift: from a simple for loop, to a more intricate repeat-while loop.

In the next chapter, we'll dig deeper and start learning how to declare and call functions, one of the most important concepts in Swift programming.

CHAPTER 5

Functions

In programming, a function is nothing but a named section of code – with or without arguments – which performs a specific task and may possibly also return a value. In this chapter, we'll see how you can get the most out of them in Swift.

5-1. Define and call a function

Problem

I want to define and call a new function from scratch.

Solution

Let's create a function sayHello.

```swift
func sayHello() {

    // This is the function 'body' - aka the statements

    print("Hello World!")
}
```

© Yanis Zafirópulos 2019

Y. Zafirópulos, *Swift 4 Recipes*, https://doi.org/10.1007/978-1-4842-4182-0_5

What about calling our function?

Note   Even without arguments, we must use parentheses

```
sayHello()
```

How It Works

Functions, by definition, are nothing but a named section of our program, usually encapsulating a specific task. Defining a function, at its simplest form, without arguments, is straightforward: we use the keyword `func`, followed by the function's name, then opening-closing parentheses (careful: that's not optional), and the function's body within curly braces.

```
Hello World!
```

5-2. Define and call a function with arguments

Problem

I want to define and call a function that takes arguments.

Solution

Let's create a function `sayHello` with takes one argument: the person whom we are going to "sayHello" to.

```
func sayHello(to: String) {

    // This is the function 'body' - aka the statements

    print("Hello \(to)!")
}
```

What about calling our function?

Note   Since our function's argument has a label ("to:"), we have to use it, even when calling it.

```
sayHello(to: "John")
```

How It Works

Defining a function with arguments is pretty much like defining a simple function, only we have to specify a list of the arguments it takes (along with their types).

```
Hello John!
```

5-3. Define and call a function with argument labels

Problem

I want to define and call a function that takes arguments with argument labels.

Solution

Let's create a function sayHello that takes one argument:

the person whom we are going to "sayHello" to.

The argument will be "person" (the variable name within the function body), but the argument label will be "to" (the way we'll call it).

```
func sayHello(to person: String) {

    // Let's say hello!

    print("Hello \(person)!")
}
```

What about calling our function?

Note   The argument label is "to," not "person," so that's what we're going to use

---

```
sayHello(to: "John")
```

How It Works

Defining a function with arguments is pretty much like defining a simple function, only we have to specify a list of the arguments it takes (along with their types). Using argument labels, we can actually define a different "calling name" for some of the parameters, so that calling a function is more expressive and "sentence-like."

```
Hello John!
```

5-4. Define and call a function without argument labels

Problem

I want to define and call a function without argument labels.

Solution

Let's create a function sayHello that takes one argument:
the person whom we are going to "sayHello" to, but this time we put an
underscore in front of it.

```
func sayHello(_ person: String) {

    // This is the function 'body' - aka the statements

    print("Hello \(person)!")
}
```

What about calling our function?

Note   Since our first argument "person:" is not a labeled one, we
omit the label – actually: we must not use any label at all – just the
parameter.

```
sayHello("John")
```

How It Works

Defining a function with arguments is pretty much like defining a simple
function, only we have to specify a list of the arguments it takes (along
with their types). However, we don't have to specify a label for each
one of them. Instead we may opt to leave one – or more – of them as
"anonymous" – using the _ syntax.

```
Hello John!
```

5-5. Define and call a function with default parameter values

Problem

I want to define and call a function, using default values.

Solution

We create a function say, which takes two arguments:

- "to": whom we are going to say something to.

- "what": what we are going to say to him.

This time this has a default value of "Hello" – meaning: if not otherwise specified, just say "Hello." It won't hurt anyway!

```
func say(to: String, what: String = "Hello") {

    // Let's say something!

    print("\(what) \(to)!")
}
```

When we call our function, we can:
- either specify only the first parameter

```
say(to: "John")
```

- or specify both of them.

```
say(to: "John", what: "Hola")
```

How It Works

Defining a function with arguments is pretty much like defining a simple function, only we have to specify a list of the arguments it takes (along with their types). Using the appropriate syntax, though, we can do even more tricks: for any parameter, a default value can be set – simply by assigning a value to the parameter after that parameter's type. This way, if a default value is defined, that parameter – when calling the function – can be omitted.

```
Hello John!
Hola John!
```

5-6. Define and call a function with return value

Problem

I want to define and call a function that returns some value.

Solution

Let's create a function that adds two numbers.

It takes two Ints as arguments, adds them up, and returns an Int – their sum.

```
func add(_ a: Int, _ b: Int) -> Int {

    // Do something with the arguments

    let sum = a + b

    // Return the result

    return sum
}
```

Now, what about using our little function?

And since it returns a value, we can use it in any expression, the same way we'd use an Int.

```
let result = add(2, 4)
```

Let's see what we've managed...

```
print("The sum of 2 and 4 is \(result)")
```

How It Works

A function, apart from performing a series of statements, may also return a value – pretty much in the way the pure "mathematical" ones do. In order to define a function with a return value, all you have to do is define it the way you'd normally do, only this time you'll have to specify its return type.

```
The sum of 2 and 4 is 6
```

5-7. Define and call a function with multiple return values

Problem

I want to define and call a function that returns multiple values.

Solution

So, let's create a function that takes two numbers and returns the result of their (integer) division, as well as the remainder.

```
func divide(_ a: Int, _ b: Int) -> (Int,Int) {
```

Divide them and get the remainder.

```
let div = a / b
let mod = a % b
```

Return the result.

```
    return (div, mod)
}
```

Now, let's try it.

```
let result = divide(13, 7)
```

Let's see what we've managed...

```
print("The division of 13/7 yields \(result)")
```

How It Works

A function, apart from performing a series of statements, may also return a value – pretty much in the way the pure "mathematical" ones do. But what if we want to return more than one value? That's where the tuples come into play!

```
The division of 13/7 yields (1, 6)
```

5-8. Call a function and ignore its return value

Problem

I want to call a function but ignore its return value.

Solution

```
func doubleIt(_ n: Int) -> Int {

    // Well, it doesn't just double our number. It first says
    'Hello!'

    print("Hello!")

    return n * 2
}
```

If we want to call it but don't need its return value, there's a little trick...

Note   Using it like doubleIt(3), like a function without a return value, the compiler will complain. So, let's do something about it and silence the warning. (It's good coding practice, too.)

```
let _ = doubleIt(3)
```

We call the function, it says "Hello!" and returns 6 but we simply choose to absolutely ignore the result.

How It Works

Let's say we have a function with a return value – which we don't actually need. How can we "ignore" it? In Swift, this can be done simply by assigning the result to _.

```
Hello!
```

5-9. Define and call a function with inout arguments

Problem

I want to define and call a function with in-out arguments, so that I can pass arguments "by reference."

Solution

That's where in-out variables come into play.

```
func sayHello(_ to: inout String) {

    // Say hello

    print("Hello \(to)!")

    // And then, change our "name" - just because we... can!

    to = "George"
}
```

Let's define a test variable.

```
var myName = "John"
```

Let's call the function.

Note   We'll do that as usual, only we'll put an & in front of the variable, in order to pass it "by reference" – so that the function can actually alter it.

```
sayHello(&myName)
```

And... let's see what happened.

```
print("My current name is: \(myName)")
```

How It Works

Defining a function with arguments means the arguments are actually constant – means we can pass whatever value we wish, but they'll never change. Nor can they change. But what if we want to call a function, send it as a variable (pass it by reference), and allow the function to manipulate and change our very variable?

In Swift, this can be done by using the inout keyword, in our function definition, and putting an & in front of the variable names we want to pass by reference, when calling it.

```
Hello John!
My current name is: George
```

5-10. Define and call a function with variadic arguments

Problem

I want to define and call a function with variadic arguments, that is: with an unspecified number of arguments.

Solution

Let's create a function that adds numbers.

"How many?," you're wondering. As many as we wish!

The only thing we have to specify is the type of the arguments. Nothing else.

```swift
func add(_ numbers: Int...) -> Int {

    // Here's where we'll be storing the total

    var total = 0;

    // Let's loop through the numbers

    for number in numbers {

        // Add them up

        total += number
    }

    // And return the result

    return total
}
```

OK, time to use to add up some numbers - the first seven Fibonacci's

```swift
let sum = add(0,1,1,2,3,5,8)
```

Finally, let's print the result.

```swift
print("The sum of the 7 Fibonacci numbers is: \(sum)")
```

How It Works

Defining a function with arguments is pretty much like defining a simple function. But what if we have a variable number of arguments, for example, we don't know how many arguments there may be, and/or we want to be prepared to use an infinite number of arguments? In Swift, this can be done by using an ellipsis (. . .) in the argument list of our function definition.

```
The sum of the 7 Fibonacci numbers is: 20
```

5-11. Define and call a function with a closure argument

Problem

I want to define and call a function that takes a closure as argument.

Solution

Let's create a test function

It takes three arguments: two numbers and a closure (the action to perform on the first two arguments).

```
func perform(_ a: Int, _ b: Int, action: (Int,Int)->Int) -> Int
{
    return action(a, b)
}
```

Let's define our "actions": one that takes two arguments and adds them up.

```
let sum = {(a: Int, b: Int) -> Int in
    return a + b
}
```

...and one that takes two arguments and returns their product.

```
let multiply = {(a: Int, b: Int) -> Int in
    return a * b
}
```

Time to test our initial function now.

```
let resultA = perform(2, 3, action: sum)
let resultB = perform(2, 3, action: multiply)
```

Let's see what we've managed.

```
print("resultA = \(resultA)")
print("resultB = \(resultB)")
```

How It Works

The same way functions can take any type as a valid argument, they can take closures as arguments, too.

```
resultA = 5
resultB = 6
```

5-12. Call a function with a trailing closure argument

Problem

I want to call a function with a trailing closure argument.

Solution

Let's create a test function.

It takes three arguments: two numbers and a closure (the action to perform on the first two arguments).

```
func perform(_ a: Int, _ b: Int, action: (Int,Int)->Int) -> Int
{
    return action(a, b)
}
```

Let's call our function with a trailing closure.

```
let sum = perform(2,3) {(a: Int, b: Int)-> Int in
    return a + b
}
```

Or using the shorthand notation:

```
let sumB = perform(2,3) { $0 + $1 }
```

Let's see what we've managed...

```
print("The sum of 2 and 3 is: \(sum)")
print("Verifying result: \(sumB)")
```

How It Works

The same way functions can take any type as a valid argument, they can take closures as arguments too. A trailing closure is the technique of writing a closure argument after the function call's parentheses, even though it is still an argument to the function.

```
The sum of 2 and 3 is: 5
Verifying result: 5
```

5-13. Define and call a function with generics

Problem

I want to define and call a function that takes arguments of a generic type, that is: without a specific already-known type.

Solution

Let's create a function that compares two items and checks if the first is greater than the second.

We'll define that "generic" type as T. So, this function of will take one argument of type... T.

```swift
func greet<T>(_ n: T) -> String {

    // Greet it...
    // no matter what it is

    return "Hello \(n)!"
}
```

Let's greet a `String`.

```swift
print(greet("John"))
```

Now, let's greet an `Int`.

```swift
print(greet(6))
```

How It Works

Defining a function with generics is pretty much like defining a simple function, except that our function won't accept arguments of a specific type. Generics are useful in the scenario when the specific type doesn't really change the main concept. For example, we can compare two Strings, as we can compare two Ints, so why have two separate functions?

```
Hello John!
Hello 6!
```

5-14. Define and call a function with generics and type constraints

Problem

I want to define and call a function that takes arguments of a generic type but with constraints, that is: without a specific already-known type but conforming to some specific protocol.

Solution

Let's create a function that compares two items and checks if the first is greater than the second.

We'll define that "generic" type as T, also mentioning that our generic types have to "obey" to the protocol Comparable. So, this function of ours takes two arguments of type... T.

```
func isGreater<T: Comparable>(_ a: T, than b: T) -> Bool {

    // if a > b, return true
    // otherwise, return false

    return a > b

}
```

Let's try our function out, with some numbers.

```
let n1 = 5
let n2 = 3

if isGreater(n1, than: n2) {
    print("n1 is greater than n2")
} else {
    print("n1 is NOT greater than n2")
}
```

Now, let's try it again, but this time with some strings.

```
let s1 = "john"
let s2 = "june"

if isGreater(s1, than: s2) {
    print("s1 is greater than s2")
} else {
    print("s1 is NOT greater than s2")
}
```

How It Works

Defining a function with generics is pretty much like defining a simple function, except that our function won't accept arguments of a specific type. Generics are useful in the scenario when the specific type doesn't really change the main concept. But what if we want our type to conform to some specific protocol? In this case, we'll be using type constraints in our argument declaration.

```
n1 is greater than n2
s1 is NOT greater than s2
```

5-15. Define and call nested functions
Problem

I want to define and call nested functions.

Solution

Let's create an example function - with two subfunctions.

Not the most... efficient way to find the difference between two numbers, but oh well...

```
func absoluteDifference(_ numA: Int, _ numB: Int) -> Int {

    // The nested functions

    func aMinB (_ a: Int, _ b: Int) -> Int { return a-b }
    func bMinA (_ a: Int, _ b: Int) -> Int { return b-a }

    // The main function body

    if numA > numB {
        return aMinB(numA, numB)
    } else {
        return bMinA(numA, numB)
    }

}
```

Let's try it.

```
let result = absoluteDifference(6,10)
```

And print out the result.

```
print("The 'distance' between 6 and 10 is: \(result)")
```

How It Works

Nested functions are nothing but functions defined within a function. Their only difference with "normal" ones is the scope: regular functions are available globally, from any part of our code, while nested ones are accessible only from inside their parent function.

```
The 'distance' between 6 and 10 is: 4
```

5-16. Summary

In this chapter, we've seen how to declare, call, and use functions in lots of different ways: from a simple barebones function, to function with arguments, argument labels, variadic arguments, or even nested ones.

In the next sections, we'll dig even deeper and start exploring the main building blocks of the Swift library: arrays, sets, dictionary, strings, and more – and how to get the most out of them.

PART II

Intermediate

CHAPTER 6

Classes and Closures

In this chapter, we're going to explore two of the most powerful elements of the Swift language: classes and closures. Classes are a neat way to group functions together, along with data, and be able to create integrated objects with "state." While closures provide us with a flexible way to use functions, without the usual function overhead – that is, defining them thoroughly, naming them, declaring their arguments, etc.

6-1. Define a basic class
Problem

We want to define a barebones class.

Solution

So, let's start, by defining a new Person class.

```
class Person {

    // When a new instance is created,
    // this is the function that gets automatically called
```

```
    init() {
        print("Hi! I feel like a new person. You just
        created me actually!")
    }
}
```

Now, let's create a new instance of this class we just defined.

```
let person = Person()
```

How It Works

Defining a new Class means basically to define a new type that encapsulates data along with functions/methods – that can perform their actions, on this data. This can be done by using Swift's `class` construct.

```
Hi! I feel like a new person. You just created me actually!
```

6-2. Define a class with instance variables
Problem

I want to define a class with instance variables.

Solution

So, let's start, by defining a new `Person` class.

```
class Person {
    // This "Person" will probably have a name right?
    var name : String
```

```
// When a new instance is created,
// this is the function that gets automatically called -
let's all set the person's name

init(_ n : String) {

        // Let's set our "name"

        name = n

        // And print something

        print("Hi! I feel like a new person. My name is: \
        (name)!")

    }
}
```

First, let's create a new instance of this class we just defined.

```
let person = Person("Nick")
```

Now, let's try to access one of our object's variables.

```
print("Hmm... your name is really \(person.name).")
```

How It Works

An instance variable is nothing but a variable defined in a class, for which each instantiated object of the class has a separate copy.

```
Hi! I feel like a new person. My name is: Nick!
Hmm... your name is really Nick.
```

6-3. Define a class with instance methods

Problem

I want to define a class with instance methods.

Solution

So, let's start, by defining a new Person class.

```
class Person {

    // This "Person" will probably have a name right?

    var name : String

    // This is the initializer method of our class

    init(_ n : String) {
        name = n
    }

    // Let's create another instance method
    // to automatically say... hello

    func sayHello() {
        print("Hello \(name)!")
    }

    // To refer to our instance variable "name", from...
    inside the class,
    // we could also use "self.name" - but only to
    differentiate it possibly from another variable, also
    called "name"
    // Usually, you won't have to use "self." that much
}
```

Now, let's create a new instance of this class we just defined.

```
let person = Person("Alicia")
```

And say hello to him!

```
person.sayHello()
```

How It Works

Instance methods are pretty much like instance variables – only they are methods. Basically, instance methods are functions defined within a class, which are able to perform their action on the class's data/variables.

```
Hello Alicia!
```

6-4. Define a class with type methods
Problem

I want to define a class with type methods.

Solution

So, let's start, by defining a new Person class.

```
class Person {

    // To define a "type" method,
    // we have to use the "class" prefix before our
    function
```

```
    class func sayHello() {

        // Let's say hello

        print("Hello everybody!")
    }

}
```

Now, let's try it out!

Careful: we're not creating a new Person object. We're just calling "sayHello" on the Person type itself.

```
Person.sayHello()
```

How It Works

Instead of instance methods (aka methods callable on instances of a particular type), we also have type methods, that is: methods that can be called on the type itself.

```
Hello everybody!
```

6-5. Define a class with default initializers
Problem

I want to define a class with default initializers.

Solution

That is: The – so-called – default initializer simply creates a new instance, with all of its properties set to their default value.

Let's create a very basic class, with some values.

```
class Vehicle {

    var numberOfWheels = 4
    var currentSpeed : Int = 0

    var brand : String?
}
```

Let's create an instance.

```
let myCar = Vehicle()
```

And print some details.

```
print("My car has \(myCar.numberOfWheels) wheels - what a
surprise!")
```

How It Works

If we want to define a (base) class without an explicit initializer method, but which includes default values for all of its properties, Swift provides us with a default initializer – that is: a way to set some initial values to our class's instance variables.

```
My car has 4 wheels - what a surprise!
```

6-6. Define a class with convenience initializers

Problem

I want to define a class with convenience initializers.

Solution

Let's create an example class.

```
class SuperNumber {

    var number : Int

    init(_ n: Int) {
        number = n
    }

    convenience init(_ s: String) {
        self.init(Int(s)!)
    }
}
```

Let's experiment a bit.

```
let a = SuperNumber(6)
let b = SuperNumber("3")
```

Time to print our super numbers.

```
print("a = \(a.number)")
print("b = \(b.number)")
```

How It Works

Convenience initializers are nothing but a shortcut to "regular" initializers, using a common initialization pattern, which will save time or make initialization more self-explanatory.

```
a = 6
b = 3
```

6-7. Define a class with initializer overloading

Problem

I want to define a class with multiple initializers.

Solution

So, let's start, by defining a new Person class.

```
class Person {

    // This "Person" will probably have a name and an age
    right?

    var name : String = "noname"
    var age  : Int = 0

    // This is the initializer method of our class - by name

    init(_ n : String) {
        name = n
    }

    // And this is a second initializer - this time, by age

    init(_ a : Int) {
        age = a
    }
}
```

Now, let's create a new instance of this class we just defined.

We can either initialize it by setting its name.

```
let personA = Person("Mary")
```

... or by setting the age

```
let personB = Person(30)
```

Finally, let's print some details about the person we created.

```
print("personA: name = \(personA.name), age = \(personA.age)")
print("personB: name = \(personB.name), age = \(personB.age)")
```

How It Works

Defining a new class with initializer overloading means a class that can be initialized with different ways, or – more precisely – via different initializer methods. Swift makes this possible in a very straightforward way: just define as many initializers as you need.

```
personA: name = Mary, age = 0
personB: name = noname, age = 30
```

6-8. Define a class with method overloading

Problem

I want to define a class with multiple methods with the same name.

Solution

So, let's start, by defining a new WeirdMath class to perform some – you guessed it – weird math!

```
class WeirdMath {

    // First we multiply a number, and return the product

    func multiply(_ x: Int, times: Int) -> Int {
        return x * times
    }

    // Then we multiply a... string (by repeating it some
    times), and return the string

    func multiply(_ x: String, times: Int) -> String {
        return String(repeating: x, count: times)
    }
}
```

Now, let's create a new instance of this class we just defined.

```
let math = WeirdMath()
```

Time to do some... weird arithmetic.

```
let a = math.multiply(3, times: 10)
let b = math.multiply("3", times: 10)
```

And let's see what we've done...

```
print("a = \(a)")
print("b = \(b)")
```

How It Works

Defining a new class with method overloading means a class that contains two (or more) different methods, with the same name, but which take different arguments. And it is most likely performing different things too. All you have to do is include the method, with as many different definitions as you wish.

```
a = 30
b = 3333333333
```

6-9. Define a class with inheritance

Problem

I want to define a class that inherits another class.

Solution

Let's define our "Parent" class – that is, a "superclass."

```
class Animal {

    var numberOfFeet = 0

    func showFeet() {
        print("I have \(numberOfFeet) feet")
    }

}
```

And then create a "child" of this type – a Dog is an animal, anyway, right? To get things straight, think of it this way:

All dogs ARE animals. But not all animals are dogs – there are plenty of different ones... but still all are considered "animals," and sharing several characteristics. Nope?

```
class Dog : Animal {

    // We use the 'override' keyword to take precedence over
    the parent class's method, with the same name

    override init() {

        // Call 'super.init' to initialize the superclass

        super.init()
```

```
            numberOfFeet = 4
    }
}
```

Let's create a new dog.

```
let myPet = Dog()
```

And try playing a bit with it...

```
print("My dog has \(myPet.numberOfFeet) feet.")
```

And again...

```
myPet.showFeet()
```

How It Works

Defining a new Class means basically to define a new type. Inheritance is a way of defining some hierarchy between types, that is: a way to group classes together, and/or help classes share common characteristics, inherit the characteristics of their parents, or "pass" their own to their children.

In Swift, to denote that a class inherits another class, all you have to do is use the Child : Parent notation.

```
My dog has 4 feet.
I have 4 feet
```

6-10. Extend an existing class
Problem

I want to extend an existing class.

Solution

So... let's play with the Int class.

```
extension Int {

    // From now on, every Int will have a "multiplyBy" method
    attached to it - ready to use!

    func multiplyBy(_ x: Int) -> Int {
        return self * x
    }

}
```

Let's see what we've managed.

```
let result = 6.multiplyBy(3)
```

Yep, it's that simple – now let's print it out to make sure.

```
print("6 * 3 = \(result)")
```

How It Works

Swift gives us the great option to extend an existing class. That is: take a class – any class, even a "system" one – and add more methods and capabilities. Great, huh? To do that all you have to do is use the extension keyword.

```
6 * 3 = 18
```

6-11. Implement and use a singleton

Problem

I want to create and use a singleton class.

Solution

```
class SharedManager {

    // Declare our 'sharedInstance' property
    static let sharedInstance = SharedManager()

    // Set an initializer and let's print something for testing
    purposes
    // Note: it will only be called once

    init() {
        print("SharedManager initialized")
    }

    // Add a test function

    func performAction() {
        print("I'm doing something important")
    }
}
```

By using SharedManager.sharedInstance, we'll always have access to
the same methods. However, only the first time it's called, it'll create a new
instance. From then on, it'll be using the existing instance we created in
the first place...

Awesome, right?

```
SharedManager.sharedInstance.performAction()
SharedManager.sharedInstance.performAction()
SharedManager.sharedInstance.performAction()
```

How It Works

Singletons are nothing but a neat programming trick to restrict the instantiation of a class to one object. This is useful when exactly one object is needed to coordinate actions across the system, and you don't want to have an endless list of instances hanging around.

```
SharedManager initialized
I'm doing something important
I'm doing something important
I'm doing something important
```

6-12. Define and use a closure

Problem

I want to define and use a closure.

Solution

Let's define a super-simple closure.

```
let sayHello = {
    print("Hello World!")
}
```

And call it – as you'd normally call any function.

```
sayHello()
```

How It Works

Closures are self-contained blocks of functionality, like Objective-C's lambdas, which can be passed around. Think of it this way: a function without a name.

```
Hello World!
```

6-13. Define and use a closure with arguments

Problem

I want to define and use a closure that takes arguments.

Solution

Let's define a super-simple closure with one argument.

```
let sayHello = {(to: String) in
    print("Hello \(to)!")
}
```

And call it – as you'd normally call any function.

Note   In contrast with "normal" functions, you must not use the argument labels.

```
sayHello("John")
```

How It Works

A closure can have arguments, as normal functions do. Why shouldn't they?

```
Hello John!
```

6-14. Define and use a closure with return value

Problem

I want to define and use a closure that returns some value.

Solution

Let's define a closure that takes two arguments and returns their sum.

```
let add = {(a: Int, b: Int)->Int in
     return a + b
}
```

Let's calculate the sum.

```
let result = add(2, 3)
```

And print it.

```
print("The sum of 2 and 3 is: \(result)")
```

How It Works

Closures can have arguments, as normal functions do. And they can also return a value – in exactly the same fashion as normal functions.

```
The sum of 2 and 3 is: 5
```

6-15. Define and use an inline closure

Problem

I want to define and use an inline closure.

Solution

'Inline' means we'll define it and use it at the same place, without the need of a separate definition.

So, let's create a closure and call it.

Note   We assign the result to _, as a way to discard it. Otherwise, the compiler will complain.

```
_ = {
    print("Hello World!")
}()
```

How It Works

Closures are self-contained blocks of functionality. Inline closures or inline expressions are an easy way of using closures, in a brief fashion, with focused syntax, but without loss of clarity.

```
Hello World!
```

6-16. Define and use an inline closure with arguments

Problem

I want to define and use an inline closure that also takes some arguments.

Solution

"Inline" means we'll define it and use it at the same place, without the need of a separate definition.

So, let's create a closure that takes two arguments and adds them up and subsequently calls it with two numbers.

```
print({(a: Int, b: Int)-> Int in
      return a+b
}(2,3))
```

How It Works

Inline closures or inline expressions are an easy way of using closures, in a brief fashion, with focused syntax, but without loss of clarity. And they can obviously have arguments too.

5

6-17. Define and use an inline closure with shorthand arguments

Problem

I want to define and use an inline closure that takes some arguments using the "shorthand" notation.

Solution

Let's see an example of a closure that takes two numbers and adds them.

```
print({(a: Int, b: Int)-> Int in
    return a+b
}(2,3))
```

Given that the types of the arguments can be inferred, this can be written as:

```
print({ a,b in a + b }(2,3))
```

Is this still too much? We can make it even shorter.

```
print({ $0 + $1 }(2,3))
```

Want even more?

Careful: not for the faint of heart, but the + operator is still a function, nope?

```
print((+)(2,3))
```

How It Works

Swift auto-magically provides us with shorthand argument names to inline closures, in order to refer to the closure's arguments, in the case where their types can be inferred. Simply put: $0 is argument number 1, $1 is argument number 2, and so on. Rather simple, nope?

```
5
5
5
5
```

6-18. Summary

In this chapter, we've looked into two of the most powerful Swift constructs: classes and closures.

In the next one, we'll start exploring bit by bit the power of Swift library, starting with one of the most used Swift objects: the String.

CHAPTER 7

Strings

In programming, a string is a way of referring to a sequence of characters, either as a literal constant or as a variable. Swift provides us with lots of functions to interact with them. In this chapter, we will dive into the Swift library for Strings and explore different ways to manipulate them efficiently.

7-1. Append character to string

Problem

I want to append a character to an existing string.

Solution

Let's initialize our Character.

```
let char : Character = "!"
```

First approach: Using the += operator.

```
var first = "Hello World"
first += String(char)

print(first)
```

© Yanis Zafirópulos 2019
Y. Zafirópulos, *Swift 4 Recipes*, https://doi.org/10.1007/978-1-4842-4182-0_7

Second approach: Using the append method.

```
var second = "Hello World"
second.append(char)

print(second)
```

How It Works

Appending a character to an existing string can be done either with the +=
operator (after converting the char to String) or using the Strings append
method – and works pretty much as with strings.

```
Hello World!
Hello World!
```

7-2. Append string to string

Problem

I want to append a string to another string.

Solution

First approach: Using the += operator.

```
var first = "Hello "
first += "World!"

print(first)
```

Second approach: Using the append method.

```
var second = "Hello "
second.append("World! - again")

print(second)
```

How It Works

Appending a string to an existing string can be done either with the +=
operator or using the Strings append method.

```
Hello World!
Hello World! - again
```

7-3. Check if object is string

Problem

I want to check if a given object is of String type.

Solution

First, we initialize our example "object" – let's make it a number.

```
var a : Any = 16
```

Now, let's see...

```
if a is String {
    print("Yes, it's a string.")
} else {
    print("Oh, no, this is not a string! Maybe it's a number?")
}
```

How It Works

To check if an object is of type String, we can use an X is String
statement. (The same construct can also be used to check whether an
object is of any other type.)

```
Oh, no, this is not a string! Maybe it's a number?
```

7-4. Check if string contains character

Problem

I want to check if a string contains a specific character.

Solution

First, we set some initial value.

```
let str = "Hello World"
let char : Character = "W"
```

Now, let's see...

```
if str.contains(char) {
    print("Well, yes, it contains the character '\(char)'...")
} else {
    print("Oops. Something went wrong!")
}
```

How It Works

In order to check if a string contains a given character, we can use the String's contains method – pretty much as we'd do with arrays.

```
Well, yes, it contains the character 'W'...
```

7-5. Check if string contains RegEx

Problem

I want to check if a string contains a given regular expression.

Solution

This method either returns the range of the regex, or `nil` - if the regex is not found.

```
import Foundation
```

First, we set some initial value.

```
let str = "Hello World"
```

Now, let's look for a digit – any digit...

```
if str.range(of: "\\d", options:.regularExpression) != nil {
    print("Yes, I found a digit...")
} else {
    print("Oops. No numbers found whatsoever...")
}
```

How It Works

In order to check if a string contains a regular expression, we can use the String's `range(of: options:)` method.

```
Oops. No numbers found whatsoever...
```

7-6. Check if string contains string

Problem

I want to check if a string contains another string.

Solution

This method either returns the range of the string, or `nil` – if the string is not found.

```
import Foundation
```

First, we set some initial value.

```
let str = "Hello World"
```

Now, let's see...

```
if str.range(of: "Hello") != nil {
    print("Well, yes, it contains the word 'Hello'...")
} else {
    print("Oops. Something went wrong!")
}
```

How It Works

In order to check if a string contains another string, we can use the Strings `range(of:)` method.

```
Well, yes, it contains the word 'Hello'...
```

7-7. Check if string ends with RegEx

Problem

I want to check if a string ends with a given regular expression.

Solution

Instead we can use the String's 'range(of:,options:)' method, along with the appropriate regular expression syntax ($).

```
import Foundation
```

First, we set some initial value.

```
let str = "Hello World"
```

Now, let's see if it ends with "World."

```
if str.range(of: "World$", options:.regularExpression) != nil {
    print("Well, yes, it ends with 'World'...")
} else {
    print("Oops. Something went wrong!")
}
```

How It Works

In order to check if a string ends with a specific regular expression, we can use its range(of:options:) method.

```
Well, yes, it ends with 'World'...
```

7-8. Check if string ends with string

Problem

I want to check if a string ends with a given string.

Solution

```
import Foundation
```

First, we set some initial value.

```
let str = "Hello World"
```

Now, let's see...

```
if str.hasSuffix("World") {
    print("Well, yes, it ends with 'World'...")
} else {
    print("Oops. Something went wrong!")
}
```

How It Works

In order to check if a string has a specific suffix, we can use the String's hasSuffix method.

```
Well, yes, it ends with 'World'...
```

7-9. Check if string is empty

Problem

I want to check if a string is empty.

Solution

First, we initialize our example string with some value.

```
let a = "Hello world!"
```

Now, let's see...

```
if a.isEmpty {
    print("Our string is empty :(")
} else {
    print("Of course it's not empty - here it is: \(a)")
}
```

How It Works

To check if a string is empty, we can use its isEmpty property.

```
Of course it's not empty - here it is: Hello world!
```

7-10. Check if string starts with RegEx
Problem

I want to check if a string starts with a regular expression.

Solution

Instead we can use the String's range(of:,options:) method, along with the appropriate regular expression syntax (^).

```
import Foundation
```

First, we set some initial value.

```
let str = "Hello World"
```

Now, let's see if it begins with "Hello."

```
if str.range(of: "^Hello", options:.regularExpression) != nil {
    print("Well, yes, it starts with 'Hello'...")
} else {
    print("Oops. Something went wrong!")
}
```

How It Works

In order to check if a string starts with a specific regular expression, we cannot use the range(of:options:) method.

```
Well, yes, it starts with 'Hello'...
```

7-11. Check if string starts with string
Problem

I want to check if a string starts with another string.

Solution

First, we set some initial value.

```
let str = "Hello World"
```

Now, let's see...

```
if str.hasPrefix("Hello") {
    print("Well, yes, it starts with 'Hello'...")
} else {
    print("Oops. Something went wrong!")
}
```

How It Works

In order to check if a string has a specific prefix, we can use the String's hasPrefix method.

```
Well, yes, it starts with 'Hello'...
```

7-12. Check if two strings are equal

Problem

I want to check if two strings are equal, that is: the same.

Solution

First, we initialize our strings.

```
let a = "first string"
let b = "second string"
```

Let's see...

```
if a == b {
    print("Yep, the strings are equal")
} else {
    print("Nope, they are different strings")
}
```

How It Works

To compare two strings and check if they are equal, we can use the == comparison operator.

```
Nope, they are different strings
```

7-13. Compare two strings

Problem

I want to compare two string lexicographically, that is: which one comes first in a dictionary.

Solution

First, we initialize our strings.

```
let a = "first string"
let b = "second string"
```

Let's see...

```
if a < b {
    print("A comes before B")
} else {
    print("B comes before A")
}
```

How It Works

To compare two strings lexicographically, we can use the < and > comparison operators.

```
A comes before B
```

7-14. Concatenate strings

Problem

I want to concatenate two different strings.

Solution

First, we set some initial values.

```
let first = "Hello "
let second = "World!"
```

Then, we concatenate them.

```
lct greeting - first + second
```

Let's see...

```
print(greeting)
```

How It Works

Concatenating two or more strings can be done, using the + operator.

```
Hello World!
```

7-15. Convert string to capitalized

Problem

I want to capitalize a given string, that is: convert the first character of each word to uppercase.

Solution

```
import Foundation
```

First, we set some initial value.

```
let str = "hello world"
```

Then, we convert it.

```
let converted = str.capitalized
```

Let's see...

```
print("'\(str)' => '\(converted)'")
```

How It Works

In order to convert a string to capitalized, that is to capitalize every single one of the words in it, we can use the String's `capitalized` property.

```
'hello world' => 'Hello World'
```

7-16. Convert string to data

Problem

I want to convert a string to a Data object.

Solution

```
import Foundation
```

First, let's set some test string.

```
let str = "This is my test string"
```

Then, we convert it to a Data object.

```
if let data = str.data(using: .utf8) {
    // And let's print it out (don't expect much!)
    print("Data: \(data)")
}
```

How It Works

In order to convert a Json string to a Data object, we may use the String's data method.

```
Data: 22 bytes
```

7-17. Convert string to double
Problem

I want to extract a value from a String as a Double.

Solution

Let's create our test string.

```
let str = "19.86"
```

Let's convert it to a Double.

```
let d = Double(str)
```

First, make sure nothing went wrong with the conversion.

```
if d != nil {
    // And print it out
    print("Result: \(d!)")
}
```

How It Works

In order to convert a String to Double, we can easily use the `Double` initializer.

```
Result: 19.86
```

7-18. Convert string to float

Problem

I want to extract a value from a String as a Float.

Solution

Let's create our test string.

```
let str = "19.86"
```

Let's convert it to a `Float`.

```
let f = Float(str)
```

First, make sure nothing went wrong with the conversion.

```
if f != nil {

    // And print it out

    print("Result: \(f!)")
}
```

How It Works

In order to convert a String to Float, we can easily use the `Float` initializer.

```
Result: 19.86
```

7-19. Convert string to integer

Problem

I want to extract a value from a String as an Int.

Solution

Let's create our test string.

```
let str = "1986"
```

Let's convert it to an Int.

```
let i = Int(str)
```

First, make sure nothing went wrong with the conversion.

```
if i != nil {
    // And print it out
    print("Result: \(i!)")
}
```

How It Works

In order to convert a String to Int, we can easily use the Int initializer.

```
Result: 1986
```

7-20. Convert string to lowercase

Problem

I want to convert a given string to lowercase.

Solution

First, we set some initial value.

```
let str = "Hello World"
```

Then, we convert it.

```
let converted = str.lowercased()
```

Let's see...

```
print("'\(str)' => '\(converted)'")
```

How It Works

In order to convert a string to lowercase, we can use the Strings `lowercased` method.

```
'Hello World' => 'hello world'
```

7-21. Convert string to uppercase
Problem

I want to convert a given string to uppercase.

Solution

First, we set some initial value.

```
let str = "Hello World"
```

Then, we convert it.

```
let converted = str.uppercased()
```

Let's see...

```
print("'\(str)' => '\(converted)'")
```

How It Works

In order to convert a string to uppercase, we can use the Strings uppercased method.

```
'Hello World' => 'HELLO WORLD'
```

7-22. Create an empty string
Problem

I want to create an empty String.

Solution

First approach: Use the "" empty string expression.

```
let a = ""
```

Second approach: Use the String initializer.

```
let b = String()
```

Let's print our two... empty strings – don't expect too much.

```
print("a: \(a), b: \(b)")
```

How It Works

In order to create an empty string, it's a piece of cake. Either initialize it, or use the String constructor.

```
a: , b:
```

7-23. Create NSString from string

Problem

I want to create a String from an NSString object.

Solution

```
import Foundation
```

First, we initialize our example string.

```
let str = "hello"
```

Let's convert it to an NSString.

```
let b = NSString(string: str)
```

Let's try using the NSString's hash property (not available for Swift pure strings), to make sure we made it.

```
print("Final string's hash: \(b.hash)")
print("Yep, it's an NSString!")
```

How It Works

In order to convert/bridge a String to an NSString, for example, when you need to access APIs that expect data in an NSString instance, or need to use some NSString-specific methods, we can use the NSString(string:) initializer.

```
Final string's hash: 17891280220473
Yep, it's an NSString!
```

7-24. Find phone number in string

Problem

I want to detect a phone number within a given String.

Solution

```
import Foundation
```

Let's set some example text.

```
let text = "This is an imaginary phone number: +34-1234567890"
```

Let's create our detector.

We want the phone numbers, so we'll look for:

```
NSTextCheckingResult.CheckingType.phoneNumber.rawValue.
```

```
let detector = try! NSDataDetector(types: NSTextCheckingResult.
CheckingType.phoneNumber.rawValue)
let results = detector.matches(in: text, options: [], range:
NSRange(location: 0, length: text.count))
```

Loop through the phone numbers we found.

```
for result in results {

    // And print them out

    print(result.phoneNumber!)

}
```

How It Works

In order to find a phone number within some text, we may use the NSDataDetector class.

```
+34-1234567890
```

7-25. Find URL in string
Problem

I want to detect a URL in a given String.

Solution

```
import Foundation
```

Let's set some example text.

```
let text = "The best site for Swift resources: https://iswift.org"
```

Let's create our detector.
We want the URLs, so we'll look for them in the following:

```
NSTextCheckingResult.CheckingType.link.rawValue.
```

```
let detector = try! NSDataDetector(types: NSTextCheckingResult.
CheckingType.link.rawValue)
let results = detector.matches(in: text, options: [], range:
NSRange(location: 0, length: text.count))
```

Loop through the URLs we found.

```
for result in results {

    // And print them out

    print(result.url!)

}
```

How It Works

In order to find a URL within some text, we may use the NSDataDetector class.

```
https://iswift.org
```

7-26. Format number in string with leading zeros
Problem

I want to format a number contained in a String, adding leading zeros.

Solution

```
import Foundation
```

First, we set our number.

```
let a = 16
let b = 2
let c = 1986
```

Now, let's format our numbers so that it has a fixed "size" of four digits and, if not, pad it with zeros.

```
let strA = String(format: "%04d", a)
let strB = String(format: "%04d", b)
let strC = String(format: "%04d", c)
```

And see what we've managed...

```
print("\(a) => \(strA)")
print("\(b) => \(strB)")
print("\(c) => \(strC)")
```

How It Works

To format a number as a string, with a number of leading zeros, we can use the String(format:_) initializer, along with the appropriate format.

```
16 => 0016
2 => 0002
1986 => 1986
```

7-27. Format number in string with specific decimal places

Problem

I want to format a number contained in a given String, specifying the number of decimal places.

Solution

```
import Foundation
```

First, we set our number.

```
let num = 3.14159265358
```

Now, let's format our number so that it has only two decimal places.

```
let str = String(format: "%.2f", num)
```

And see what we've managed...

```
print("Result: \(str)")
```

How It Works

To format a number – float or double – as a string, with a specific number of decimal places, we can use the `String(format:_)` initializer, along with the appropriate format.

```
Result: 3.14
```

7-28. Format string by padding left with spaces

Problem

I want to format a given string by adding some left padding, with a number of spaces.

Solution

First, we set our string.

```
let str = "Hello World"
```

Now, let's format our string so that it has a fixed "size" of 25, and – if not – pad it with spaces at the left.

```
let padded = String(repeating: " ", count: 25-str.count) + str
```

And print the result.

```
print("Result: |\(padded)|")
```

How It Works

To format a string with a number of spaces at the left, we can use the String's `String(repeating:count:)` initializer, along with the necessary string manipulation.

```
Result: |              Hello World|
```

7-29. Format string by padding right with spaces

Problem

I want to format a given string by adding some right padding, with a number of spaces.

Solution

```
import Foundation
```

First, we set our string.

```
let str = "Hello World"
```

Now, let's format our string so that it has a fixed "size" of 25, and – if not – pad it with spaces at the right.

```
let padded = str.padding(toLength: 25, withPad: " ",
startingAt: 0)
```

And print the result.

```
print("Result: |\(padded)|")
```

How It Works

To format a string with a number of spaces at the right, we can use the String's `padding(toLength:withPad:startingAt:)` method.

```
Result: |Hello World              |
```

7-30. Generate a unique identifier string

Problem

I want to generate a UUID string.

Solution

```
import Foundation
```

A single line does the trick.

```
let uuid = UUID().uuidString
```

Let's print it out...

```
print(uuid)
```

How It Works

A UUID is a universally unique identifier, and there's surely an easy way to generate one. How? By using Foundation's UUID class.

```
9A4EE9F3-772D-4A17-A213-0828E9E7742A
```

7-31. Get character at index in string

Problem

I want to get the character at specific index of a given String.

Solution

```
import Foundation
```

Let's initialize a test string.

```
let str = "Hello world"
```

We want the character at index: 6.

First, we get the index.

```
let index = str.index(str.startIndex, offsetBy: 6)
```

Then we retrieve the character.

```
let char = str[index]
```

Let's see what we've managed...

```
print("Character at index 6: \(char)")
```

How It Works

To get a particular character at a specific index of a string, we'll have to use the String's index(_,offsetBy:) method and then subscript.

```
Character at index 6: w
```

7-32. Get first X characters from string

Problem

I want to get the first characters from a given String.

Solution

First, we initialize a test string.

```
let str = "Hello world!!!"
```

We want the string from the beginning of the string up to index: 5.

```
let indexFrom = str.startIndex
let indexTo = str.index(str.startIndex, offsetBy:5)
```

Then we retrieve the substring.

```
let substring = str[indexFrom..<indexTo]
```

Let's see...

```
print(substring)
```

How It Works

In order to get the first X characters of a string (the substring), we can use the subscript and the String's index(_,offsetBy:) method.

```
Hello
```

7-33. Get index of character in string
Problem

I want to get the index of a specific character within a given String.

Solution

First, we initialize a test string.

```
let str = "Hello world"
```

Then, we get the index of 'l'.
Careful: we have lots of 'l's in the string. This way we'll get the index of the first one.

```
let index = str.index(of: "l")
```

Index is an optional. Meaning: it's not guaranteed that we'll find the character. So, let's first check if we did find the character.

```
if index != nil {

    // Now, let's convert the index to an Int

    let intIndex : Int = str.distance(from: str.startIndex,
    to: index!)

    // And print it out

    print("First 'l' found at index: \(intIndex)")
}
```

How It Works

To get the index of the first occurrence of a specific character within a string, we can use index(of:) the method of its characters property.

```
First 'l' found at index: 2
```

7-34. Get index of substring in string

Problem

I want to get the index of a string within a given String.

Solution

```
import Foundation
```

First, we initialize a test string.

```
let str = "Hello world"
```

Then, we get the range of "world."

```
let range = str.range(of: "world")
```

Range is an optional. Meaning: it's not guaranteed that we'll find the substring. So, let's first check if we did find the substring.

```
if range != nil {

    // First, let's get the initial index - or "lower bound"
    of the string's range

    let index = range!.lowerBound

    // Now, let's convert the index to an Int

    let intIndex : Int = str.distance(from: str.startIndex,
    to: index)

    // And print it out

    print("String 'world' found at position: \(intIndex)")
}
```

How It Works

To get the index of the first occurrence of a specific string within a string, we can use the range(of:) method.

```
String 'world' found at position: 6
```

7-35. Get last X characters from string
Problem

I want to get the last characters from a given String.

Solution

First, we initialize a test string.

```
let str = "Hello world!!!"
```

We want the string from index: 6 to the end of the string.

```
let indexFrom = str.index(str.startIndex, offsetBy:6)
let indexTo = str.endIndex
```

Then we retrieve the substring.

```
let substring = str[indexFrom..<indexTo]
```

Let's see...

```
print(substring)
```

How It Works

In order to get the last X characters of a string (the substring), we can use the subscript and the String's index(_,offsetBy:) method.

```
world!!!
```

7-36. Get length of string

Problem

I want to get the length of a given String.

Solution

So, let's initialize some test string.

```
let str = "Hello World"

let length = str.count
```

Let's see...

```
print("Number of characters in the string: \(length)")
```

How It Works

To get the length of the string, all we have to use String's count property.

```
Number of characters in the string: 11
```

7-37. Get length of Unicode string

Problem

I want to get the length of a Unicode String.

Solution

So, to get the length of the string, we'd do as with a normal string: all we have to do is get the string's characters and count them. Literally.

So, let's initialize some test string.

That's "Japanese." In, well... Japanese.

```
let str = "日本語"

let length = str.count
```

Let's see...

```
print("Number of characters in the string: \(length)")
```

How It Works

In Swift, using Unicode characters in string, works practically out of the box.

```
Number of characters in the string: 3
```

7-38. Get substring from string in range

Problem

I want to get a specific substring, from a specific range, within a given String.

Solution

First, we initialize a test string.

```
let str = "Hello world!!!"
```

We want the string from index: 6 to index: 11.

```
let indexFrom = str.index(str.startIndex, offsetBy:6)
let indexTo = str.index(str.startIndex, offsetBy:11)
```

Then we retrieve the substring.

```
let substring = str[indexFrom..<indexTo]
```

Let's see...

```
print(substring)
```

How It Works

In order to get a substring, from a string, given a specific range, we can use the subscript and for the different index the Strings index(_,offsetBy:) method.

```
world
```

7-39. Loop through characters in string

Problem

I want to iterate over the characters contained in a given String.

Solution

Let's initialize our string with some value.

```
let str = "Hello World!"
```

Iterate through the characters, with a for-in statement.

```
for char in str {
    print(char)
}
```

How It Works

To get the characters in a string, we may just iterate over the String itself using a for-in statement.

```
H
e
l
l
o
```

```
W
o
r
l
d
!
```

7-40. Repeat a string several times

Problem

I want to repeat a given String several times.

Solution

First, set an initial test string.

```
let str = "x"
```

Now, let's repeat it three times.

```
let repeated = String(repeating: str, count: 3)
```

Let's see...

```
print("\(str) => \(repeated)")
```

How It Works

In order to repeat a string several times and create a new string, we can use the String(repeating: count:) initializer.

```
x => xxx
```

7-41. Check if string starts with string

Problem

I want to check if a String starts with another String.

Solution

```
import Foundation
```

First, we set some initial value.

```
var str = "Hello world"
```

We're going to replace the first space.

```
if let subrange = str.range(of: "\\s", options:.
regularExpression) {
        // Replace the substring with 'Hola'
        str.replaceSubrange(subrange, with: "_")
        // And print it
        print("Here is our new string: \(str)")
}
```

How It Works

In order to replace a regex within a string, we can use the Strings range(of:) method to first find its range, and then replaceSubrange (_,with:) in order to replace it.

```
Here is our new string: Hello_world
```

7-42. Replace substring in string by range

Problem

I want to replace a String within another String, given a specific range.

Solution

```
import Foundation
```

First, we set some initial value.

```
var str = "Hello World!!!"
```

We'll want to replace everything from index: 6 up to index: 11.

```
let indexFrom = str.index(str.startIndex, offsetBy:6)
let indexTo = str.index(str.startIndex, offsetBy:11)
```

Time to replace it.

```
str.replaceSubrange(indexFrom..<indexTo, with: "Mundo")
```

And print it.

```
print("Here is our new string: \(str)")
```

How It Works

In order to replace a substring within a string, given a specific range, we can use the String's range(of:) method to first find its range, and then replaceSubrange(_,with:) in order to replace it.

```
Here is our new string: Hello Mundo!!!
```

7-43. Replace substring in string

Problem

I want to replace a String within another String.

Solution

```
import Foundation
```

First, we set some initial value.

```
var str = "Hello World"
```

Now, let's see...

```
if let subrange = str.range(of: "Hello") {
    // Replace the substring with 'Hola'
    str.replaceSubrange(subrange, with: "Hola")
    // And print it
    print("Here is our new string: \(str)")
}
```

How It Works

In order to replace a substring within a string, we can use the String's range(of:) method to first find its range, and then replaceSubrange(_,with:) in order to replace it.

```
Here is our new string: Hola World
```

7-44. Reverse a string
Problem

I want to reverse a String.

Solution

First, we set some initial value.

```
let str = "Hello World"
```

Time to reverse it.

```
let reversed = String(str.reversed())
```

Let's see...

```
print("\(str) => \(reversed)")
```

How It Works

In order to reverse a string, we can use the String's reversed method.

```
Hello World => dlroW olleH
```

7-45. Split string by lines
Problem

I want to split a given String into lines.

Solution

```
import Foundation
```

First, we set some initial value.

```
let str = "bananas\n" +
          "apples\n" +
          "apricots\n" +
          "pineapples\n" +
          "oranges"
```

Let's split it by lines, and get the different types of fruit.

```
let lines = str.components(separatedBy: "\n")
```

Let's see...

```
print(lines)
```

How It Works

In order to split a string by lines, we can use the String's `components(separatedBy:)` method.

```
["bananas", "apples", "apricots", "pineapples", "oranges"]
```

7-46. Split string by words
Problem

I want to split a given String by words.

Solution

```
import Foundation
```

First, let's set some test string.

```
let str = "The quick brown fox jumps over the lazy dog"
```

Then, we set up our tagger – it can do LOTS more than just split our string to words, but let's stick to that for now.

```
let options = NSLinguisticTagger.Options.omitWhitespace

let tagger = NSLinguisticTagger(tagSchemes:
[NSLinguisticTagScheme.lexicalClass],

                                    options:
Int(options.rawValue))

tagger.string = str
```

Time to loop through the tokens found.

```
var words : [String] = []

tagger.enumerateTags(in: NSMakeRange(0, (str as NSString).
length), scheme: NSLinguisticTagScheme.lexicalClass, options:
options) {
        (tag, tokenRange, _, _) in

    let token = (str as NSString).substring(with:
    tokenRange)
    words.append(token)
  }
```

Let's print the words.

```
print("Words: \(words)")
```

How It Works

In order to split a string by words, the best way would be by using the NSLinguisticTagger class.

Words: ["The", "quick", "brown", "fox", "jumps", "over", "the", "lazy", "dog"]

7-47. Split string into array by separator

Problem

I want to split a given String into an array using a specific separator.

Solution

```
import Foundation
```

First, we set some initial value.

```
let str = "bananas,apples,apricots,pineapples,oranges"
```

Let's split it by commas, and get the different types of fruit.

```
let fruit = str.components(separatedBy: ",")
```

Let's see...

```
print(fruit)
```

How It Works

In order to split a string into an array, we can use the String's components(separatedBy:) method.

["bananas", "apples", "apricots", "pineapples", "oranges"]

7-48. Trim characters in string

Problem

I want to trim characters in a given String.

Solution

```
import Foundation
```

First, we set some initial value.

```
let str = "this is our string"
```

We want to "trim" all 't's and 'g's.

```
let toTrim = CharacterSet(charactersIn: "tg")
let trimmed = str.trimmingCharacters(in: toTrim)
```

Let's see...

```
print(": \(trimmed) :")
```

How It Works

In order to remove several characters from the beginning and end of a string, we can use the String's trimmingCharacters(in:).

```
: his is our strin :
```

7-49. Trim whitespace in string

Problem

I want to trim all whitespace in a given String.

Solution

```
import Foundation
```

First, we set some initial value.

```
let str = "  This is a string with some... space around    "
```

Then, we convert it.

```
let trimmed = str.trimmingCharacters(in:
.whitespacesAndNewlines)
```

Let's see...

```
print(": \(trimmed) :")
```

How It Works

In order to remove all whitespace (and newlines) from the beginning and end of a string, we can use the String's trimmingCharacters(in:) method.

```
: This is a string with some... space around :
```

7-50. Use string interpolation

Problem

I want to "include" an expression – string, number or whatever-that-may-be – within a String literal.

Solution

On the more... technical side, what string interpolation does is to embed the *string representation* (think of the description method) of a particular expression within another string.

128

Let's set some initial variables.

```
let str = "hello"
let num = 6
let arr = [1,9,8,6] // yep, arrays too!
```

Now, let's see it in action.

```
print("str = \(str)")
print("num = \(num)")
print("arr = \(arr)")
```

This is not limited to variables; you can actually use any expression.

```
print("str uppercased = \(str.uppercased())")
print("num after addition = \(num + 4)")
print("arr after sorting = \(arr.sorted())")
```

How It Works

First, let's set things straight: String interpolation is just a way to "include" an expression – string, number, whatever-that-may-be – within a string. That's all. So, instead of concatenating string after string... you can just use the \(..) syntax to just embed it.

```
str = hello
num = 6
arr = [1, 9, 8, 6]
str uppercased = HELLO
num after addition = 10
arr after sorting = [1, 6, 8, 9]
```

7-51. Use Unicode characters in string

Problem

I want to include Unicode characters in a String literal.

Solution

Let's create some strings.

```
let a = "日本語 = Japanese"
let b = "You really \u{2665} Swift, don't you?"
```

Let's print them out.

```
print("a: \(a)")
print("b: \(b)")
```

How It Works

In Swift, using Unicode characters in string works practically out of the box.

```
a: 日本語 = Japanese
b: You really ♥ Swift, don't you?
```

7-52. Summary

In this chapter, we've seen how to make the most out of our Strings in Swift.

In the next chapter, we'll dig deeper and start exploring yet another one of the most fundamental objects in the Swift programming language: arrays and sets.

CHAPTER 8

Arrays and Sets

In programming, an array or a set is nothing but a collection of items/objects – in the case of arrays, also of the same type. Swift, apart from allowing us to store our object in an array or a set, offers us a wide range of functions and methods to manipulate them. In this chapter, we'll explore the vast capabilities of the Swift libraries and find ways to make the most out of our object collections.

8-1. Append array to array
Problem

I want to append an array to an existing array.

Solution

Let's initialize our array.

```swift
var a = [1,2,3]
var b = [4,5,6]
```

And append the new array.

```swift
a += b
```

© Yanis Zafirópulos 2019
Y. Zafirópulos, *Swift 4 Recipes*, https://doi.org/10.1007/978-1-4842-4182-0_8

Let's print out the resulting arrays (Array 'b' will be exactly the same – we didn't do anything to it, did we?)

```
print("a: \(a)")
print("b: \(b)")
```

How It Works

Appending an array to an existing array can be done with the += operator.

```
a: [1, 2, 3, 4, 5, 6]
b: [4, 5, 6]
```

8-2. Append item to array

Problem

I want to append an item to an existing array.

Solution

First approach: Using the += operator.

```
var first = [1,2,3]
first += [4]

print("First: \(first)")
```

Second approach: Using the append method.

```
var second = [1,2,3]
second.append(4)

print("Second: \(second)")
```

How It Works

Appending an item to an existing array can be done either with the +=
operator or using the Array's append method.

```
First: [1, 2, 3, 4]
Second: [1, 2, 3, 4]
```

8-3. Check if array contains item

Problem

I want to check if an array contains a specific item.

Solution

First, we initialize our example array with some values.

```
let a = [1,2,3]
```

Now, let's see...

```
if a.contains(3) {
    print("Yes, our array contains the number 3")
} else {
    print("Nope, the array doesn't contain the number 3")
}
```

How It Works

To check if an array contains a particular element, we can use its contains
method.

```
Yes, our array contains the number 3
```

8-4. Check if array is empty

Problem

I want to check if an array is empty.

Solution

First, we initialize our example array with some values.

```
let a = [1,2,3]
```

Now, let's see...

```
if a.isEmpty {
    print("Our array is empty :(")
} else {
    print("Of course it's not empty - we just created it!")
}
```

How It Works

To check if an array is empty, we can use its isEmpty property.

```
Of course it's not empty - we just created it!
```

8-5. Check if object is array

Problem

I want to check if an object is of type Array.

Solution

First, we initialize our example "object" – let's make it an array, as expected.

```
var a : Any = [1,2,3]
```

Now, let's see...

```
if a is [Int] {
    print("Yes, it's an integer array. Yay!")
} else {
    print("Oh, no, this is not an array!")
}
```

How It Works

To check if an object is of type Array, we can use an X is Array or X is [type] statement.

```
Yes, it's an integer array. Yay!
```

8-6. Check if two arrays are equal

Problem

I want to check if two different arrays are equal.

Solution

First, we initialize our arrays.

```
let a = [1,2,3]
let b = [4,5,6]
```

Let's see...

```
if a == b {
    print("Yep, the arrays are equal")
} else {
    print("Nope, they are different arrays")
}
```

How It Works

To compare two arrays and check if they are equal, we can use the ==
comparison operator.

```
Nope, they are different arrays
```

8-7. Check if two tuples are equal
Problem

I want to check if two different tuples are equal.

Solution

First, we initialize our tuples.

```
let a = (1, "one")
let b = (2, "two")
```

Let's see...

```
if a == b {
    print("Yep, the tuples are equal")
} else {
    print("Nope, they are different tuples")
}
```

How It Works

To compare two tuples and check if they are equal, we can use the == comparison operator.

```
Nope, they are different tuples
```

8-8. Combine two arrays into array of tuples

Problem

I want to combine two different arrays into an array of tuples, with the elements from both of the initial arrays.

Solution

Let's initialize our test arrays.

```
let english = ["one", "two", "three", "four", "five"]
let spanish = ["uno", "dos", "tres", "cuatro", "cinco"]
```

Time to combine them.

```
let result = zip(english, spanish).map { ($0,$1) }
```

Let's see the resulting array...

```
print("Result: \(result)")
```

How It Works

If we have two different arrays and want to combine their elements in pairs, we can use the zip function and then map the resulting pairs into an array of tuples.

```
Result: [("one", "uno"), ("two", "dos"), ("three", "tres"),
("four", "cuatro"), ("five", "cinco")]
```

8-9. Combine two arrays into dictionary

Problem

I want to combine two different arrays into one dictionary, containing the elements from both of the initial arrays, in the form of key-value pairs.

Solution

Let's initialize our test arrays.

```
let english = ["one", "two", "three", "four", "five"]
let spanish = ["uno", "dos", "tres", "cuatro", "cinco"]
```

And a dictionary to hold our "glossary."

```
var glossary : [String:String] = [:]
```

Time to combine them.

```
zip(english, spanish).forEach { glossary[$0] = $1 }
```

Let's see the resulting dictionary...

```
print("Result: \(glossary)")
```

How It Works

If we have two different arrays and want to combine their elements into a dictionary, we can use the zip function and then *map* the resulting pairs into key-value pairs of a dictionary.

```
Result: ["three": "tres", "four": "cuatro", "five": "cinco",
"one": "uno", "two": "dos"]
```

8-10. Concatenate arrays

Problem

I want to concatenate two different arrays.

Solution

First, we set some initial values.

```
let first = [1,2,3]
let second = [4,5,6]
```

Then, we concatenate them.

```
let result = first + second
```

Let's see...

```
print(result)
```

How It Works

Concatenating two or more arrays can be done, using the + operator.

```
[1, 2, 3, 4, 5, 6]
```

8-11. Convert array to enumerated sequence

Problem

I want to convert an array to an enumerated sequence.

Solution

First, we initialize our example array with some values.

```
let arr = ["one", "two", "three", "four"]
```

Let's convert it to an enumerated sequence.

```
let enumerated = arr.enumerated()
```

Let's print it out.

```
for (index,item) in enumerated {
    print("\(index) => \(item)")
}
```

How It Works

In order to convert an array to an enumerated sequence, that is: a sequence of (n, x) pairs, where n represents a consecutive integer starting at zero, and x represents an element of the sequence, we can use the Array's enumerated method.

```
0 => one
1 => two
2 => three
3 => four
```

8-12. Convert array to JSON string

Problem

I want to convert an array to its JSON string representation.

Solution

```
import Foundation
```

First, let's create an example array.

```
let arr : [Any] = [ 1, "Banana", 2, "Apple", 3, "Orange", 4,
"Apricot" ]

do {

    // Convert our array to JSON data

    let json = try JSONSerialization.data(withJSONObject:
    arr, options: .prettyPrinted)

    // Convert our JSON data to string

    let str = String(data: json, encoding: .utf8)

    // And if all went well, print it out

    print(str ?? "Ooops... Error converting JSON to string!")

}
catch let error
{
    print("Error: \(error)")
}
```

How It Works

In order to convert a Swift Array to JSON, we may use the
`JSONSerialization` class.

```
[
  1,
  "Banana",
  2,
  "Apple",
  3,
  "Orange",
  4,
  "Apricot"
]
```

8-13. Convert JSON string to array

Problem

I want to convert a JSON string representation to an Array object.

Solution

```
import Foundation
```

First, let's set some test JSON.

```
let json = "[ 1, \"Banana\", 2, \"Apple\", 3, \"Orange\", 4,
\"Apricot\" ]"
```

Then, we convert it to a Data object.

```
if let data = json.data(using: .utf8) {

    // if everything went fine,
    // it's time to convert our Data object to an Array

    let result = try? JSONSerialization.jsonObject(with:
    data, options: []) as! [Any]

    // And finally, what about printing out our array?

    print(result ?? "Ooops... Error converting JSON!")

}
```

How It Works

In order to convert a JSON string to a Swift Array, we may use the JSONSerialization class.

```
[1, Banana, 2, Apple, 3, Orange, 4, Apricot]
```

8-14. Create a string from character array
Problem

I want to create a String object from a given Character Array.

Solution

First, we initialize our Character array.

```
let arr : [Character] = ["H", "e", "l", "l", "o", "!"]
```

Convert it to a string, using the `String` initializer.

```
let str = String(arr)
```

Let's see what we've managed...

```
print(str)
```

How It Works

Technically, a string is nothing but a sequence/array of characters. So, we can also create a string from a pure array of characters.

```
Hello!
```

8-15. Create an array from range

Problem

I want to create an array from a given range.

Solution

First, let's say we want all numbers from 0 up to 4 (including 4).

```
let a = Array(0...4)
```

Then, let's say we want all numbers from 6 up to 9 (but not including 9).

```
let b = Array(6..<9)
```

Time to print out our arrays.

```
print("a: \(a)")
print("b: \(b)")
```

How It Works

Creating an array from a range is as simple as using the `Array` initializer along with the desired range.

```
a: [0, 1, 2, 3, 4]
b: [6, 7, 8]
```

8-16. Create an array from stride

Problem

I want to create an array from a given stride.

Solution

First, let's say we want all numbers from 0 up to 10 (not including 10), with a step of 2 - that is: don't take all of them, just every 2 of them.

```
let s = stride(from: 0, to: 10, by: 2)
```

Now, let's convert it to an array.

```
let a = Array(s)
```

...and print it out.

```
print("a: \(a)")
```

How It Works

Creating an array from a Stride is as simple as using the `Array` initializer along with the desired stride.

```
a: [0, 2, 4, 6, 8]
```

8-17. Create an array with literal

Problem

I want to create an array from an Array literal.

Solution

This is an array, with its type automatically inferred.

```
let a = ["one", "two", "three"]
```

This is another one, but this time let's set a type.

```
let b : [String] = ["un", "dos", "tres"]
```

Let's create a mixed array with different types of elements. This time we have to explicitly say it's of type [Any]. Otherwise, the compiler will doubt whether that was our intention.

```
let c : [Any] = ["one", 1, "two", 2]
```

Let's see what we've managed...

```
print("a: \(a), b: \(b), c: \(c)")
```

How It Works

Creating an array from an array literal is as simple as listing your values, separated by commas, surrounded by a pair of square brackets ([..]).

```
a: ["one", "two", "three"], b: ["un", "dos", "tres"], c:
["one", 1, "two", 2]
```

8-18. Create an empty array

Problem

I want to create an empty Array object.

Solution

First approach: Use the [ ] empty array expression.

```
let a : [Int] = []
```

Second approach: Use an Array constructor.

```
let b = [String]()
```

Third approach: "Enforce" its type with as.

```
let c = [] as [Any]
```

Let's print our three... empty arrays.

```
print("a: \(a), b: \(b), c: \(c)")
```

How It Works

In order to create an empty array, the only thing you have to specify is the *type* of items it's going to contain. That is String, Int, or... anything.

```
a: [], b: [], c: []
```

8-19. Create NSArray from Array

Problem

I want to create an NSArray object from a given array.

Solution

```
import Foundation
```

First, we initialize our example array with some values.

```
let arr = [1, 2, 3, 4]
```

Let's convert it to an NSArray.

```
let b = NSArray(array: arr)
```

Let's try using the NSArray's 'hash' property (not available for Swift pure arrays) to make sure we made it.

```
print("Final array's hash: \(b.hash)")
print("Yep, it's an NSArray!")
```

How It Works

In order to convert/bridge an Array to an NSArray, for example, when you need to access APIs that expect data in an NSArray instance, we can use the NSArray(array:) initializer.

```
Final array's hash: 4
Yep, it's an NSArray!
```

8-20. Create set from array literal
Problem

I want to create a set from an Array literal.

Solution

Let's initialize our set.

```
let a : Set = ["one", "two", "three"]
```

We may also explicitly declare its element's type.

```
let b : Set<String> = ["uno", "dos", "tres"]
```

Let's see what we've managed...

```
print("a: \(a), b: \(b)")
```

How It Works

Creating a set from array works pretty much like initializing an array.
That is: listing your values, separated by commas, surrounded by a pair of
square brackets ([..]).

```
a: ["one", "three", "two"], b: ["tres", "uno", "dos"]
```

8-21. Filter an array by condition
Problem

I want to filter a given array's elements by a specific condition.

Solution

First, we initialize our test array.

```
let numbers = [1, 2, 3, 4, 5, 6, 7, 8, 9, 10]
```

Let's keep only the odd numbers.

```
let odd = numbers.filter { $0 % 2 == 1}
```

And... print the result.

```
print("The odd numbers only: \(odd)")
```

How It Works

If we have an array and want to filter some of its elements based on some condition, then we can use the Array's `filter` method along with the appropriate closure.

```
The odd numbers only: [1, 3, 5, 7, 9]
```

8-22. Get array element at index

Problem

I want to get an array element at a specific index.

Solution

First, we initialize a test array.

```
let arr = ["one", "two", "three"]
```

We want the item at index: 1.

```
let item = arr[1]
```

Let's see...

```
print("Item at index 1: \(item)")
```

How It Works

To get a particular element at a specific index of an array, we may use its *subscript*.

```
Item at index 1: two
```

8-23. Get array of values in dictionary

Problem

I want to retrieve the values in a given dictionary as an array.

Solution

Let's initialize our test dictionary.

```
let dict = [
    "name"          : "John",
    "surname"      : "Doe",
    "email"          : "info@iswift.org"
]
```

Then, we get its values into an array.

```
let values = Array(dict.values)
```

Let's print the result...

```
print("Our dictionary values: \(values)")
```

How It Works

A dictionary is a collection of key-value pairs. But what if we want to get just the values? For that, we can use the Dictionary's `values` property.

```
Our dictionary values: ["John", "Doe", "info@iswift.org"]
```

8-24. Get array valid indices

Problem

I want to get an array of valid indices for a given array.

Solution

First, we initialize our example array with some values.

```
var a = [1, 2, 3, 4]
```

Let's remove the last elements.

```
let indices = a.indices
```

Let's see...

```
print("The array's valid indices: \(indices)")
```

How It Works

To check an array's valid indices, that is: the indices that are valid for subscripting the collection, we can use the Array's `indices` property.

```
The array's valid indices: 0..<4
```

8-25. Get capacity of array

Problem

I want to get the total capacity of a given array.

Solution

First, we initialize our example array with some values.

```
var a = [1, 2, 3, 4]
```

Let's remove the last elements.

```
let _ = a.removeLast()
```

Let's now check the array's capacity.

Note   The capacity of an array is not necessarily the same as the number of elements it currently contains.

```
let capacity = a.capacity

print("The array's capacity: \(capacity)")
```

How It Works

To check the capacity of an array, that is: the total number of elements that the array can contain using its current storage, we can use the Array's capacity property.

```
The array's capacity: 4
```

8-26. Get element index in array by value

Problem

I want to get the index of a specific element in a given array by its value.

Solution

First, we initialize a test array.

```
let arr = ["one", "two", "three"]
```

We want the item at index: 1.

```
let index = arr.index(of: "two")
```

If we found it, let's print its index.

```
if let i = index {
    print("Item 'two' is at index: \(i)")
}
```

How It Works

To get the index of a particular element – based on its value – we may use the Array's index(of:) method.

```
Item 'two' is at index: 1
```

8-27. Get first item from array

Problem

I want to get an array's first element.

Solution

First, we initialize a test array.

```
let arr = ["one", "two", "three"]
```

First approach: Do it with the subscript.

```
let a = arr[0]
```

Second approach: Use the `first` property.

Note   This one returns an optional.

```
let b = arr.first ?? "error"
```

Let's print out the results...

```
print("a: \(a), b: \(b)")
```

How It Works

To get the first element in an array, we may use either the subscript or the Array's `first` property.

```
a: one, b: Optional("one")
```

8-28. Get first X items from array

Problem

I want to retrieve the first elements from a given array.

Solution

First, we initialize a test array.

```
let arr = ["one", "two", "three", "four", "five"]
```

Let's get the first three items.

```
let slice = arr.prefix(3)
```

Let's print out the results...

```
print("slice: \(slice)")
```

How It Works

To get the first X elements in an array, we may use the Array's `prefix` method.

```
slice: ["one", "two", "three"]
```

8-29. Get index of item in array

Problem

I want to get the index of a specific item in a given array.

Solution

First, we initialize a test array.

```
let arr = ["one", "two", "three", "one", "two", "four"]
```

Then, we get the index of "two."

```
let index = arr.index(of: "two")
```

We must first check that we did find it.

```
if index != nil {

    // Let's print out the result

    print("First 'two' found at index: \(index!)")
}
```

How It Works

To get the index of the first occurrence of a specific item within an array, we may use the index(of:) method.

```
First 'two' found at index: 1
```

8-30. Get indices of item in array
Problem

I want to get the indices (if more than one) of a specific item in a given array.

Solution

First, we initialize a test array.

```
let arr = ["one", "two", "three", "one", "two", "four"]
```

Let's set an array where we'll keep our indices.

```
var indices : [Int] = []
```

Time to loop through our array and look for 'two's.

```
for (index,item) in arr.enumerated() {

    // If it's the item we're looking for,
    // add it to our 'indices' array

    if item == "two" { indices.append(index) }
}
```

Let's print out the result...

```
print("'two' found at indices: \(indices)")
```

How It Works

To get the indices of all occurrences of a specific item within an array, we may loop through the array, and check the items one by one.

```
'two' found at indices: [1, 4]
```

8-31. Get last item from array
Problem

I want to get the last element of a given array.

Solution

First, we initialize a test array.

```
let arr = ["one", "two", "three"]
```

First approach: Do it with the subscript.

```
let a = arr[arr.count-1]
```

Second approach: Use the `last` property.

Note   This one returns an optional.

```
let b = arr.last
```

Let's print out the results...

```
print("a: \(a), b: \(String(describing:b))")
```

How It Works

To get the last element in an array, we may use either the *subscript* or the Array's `last` property.

```
a: three, b: Optional("three")
```

8-32. Get last X items from array

Problem

I want to retrieve the last elements from a given array.

Solution

First, we initialize a test array.

```
let arr = ["one", "two", "three", "four", "five"]
```

Let's get the last three items.

```
let slice = arr.suffix(3)
```

Let's print out the results...

```
print("slice: \(slice)")
```

How It Works

To get the last X elements in an array, we may use the Array's `suffix` method.

```
slice: ["three", "four", "five"]
```

8-33. Get maximum value in array

Problem

I want to retrieve the maximum value from a number array.

Solution

First, we initialize a test array.

```
let arr = [1,2,3,4,5,6]
```

Then we get the maximum item.

Note   This returns an optional.

```
let m = arr.max()
```

Let's find out...

```
print("Maximum: \(String(describing:m))")
```

How It Works

To get the maximum element in an array, we may use the Array's `max` method.

```
Maximum: Optional(6)
```

8-34. Get minimum value in array

Problem

I want to retrieve the minimum value from a number array.

Solution

First, we initialize a test array.

```
let arr = [1,2,3,4,5,6]
```

Then we get the minimum item.

Note   This returns an optional.

```
let m = arr.min()
```

Let's find out...

```
print("Minimum: \(String(describing:m))")
```

How It Works

To get the minimum element in an array, we may use the Array's min method.

```
Minimum: Optional(1)
```

8-35. Get random item from array

Problem

I want to retrieve a random element from a given array.

Solution

```
import Foundation
```

First, we initialize a test array.

```
var fruit = ["pineapple", "banana", "apple", "mango", "apricot"]
```

Then, we get a random fruit from our basket.

```
var rnd = Int(arc4random()) % fruit.count
var randomFruit = fruit[rnd]
```

Let's print it out...

```
print("Here's the fruit I picked for you: \(randomFruit)")
```

How It Works

To get a random element from an array, we'll be using the arc4random function.

```
Here's the fruit I picked for you: apple
```

8-36. Get size of array
Problem

I want to get the size of a given array.

Solution

First, we initialize our example array with some values.

```
let a = [1,2,3]
```

Now, let's count how many items we've got.

```
print("The array contains \(a.count) elements")
```

How It Works

To check the size of an array, we can use its count property.

```
The array contains three elements
```

8-37. Get tuple element by index
Problem

I want to retrieve a tuple element by its index.

Solution

First, we initialize a test tuple.

```
let tuple = ("one", "two", "three")
```

We want the item at index: 1.

```
let item = tuple.1
```

Let's see...

```
print("Item at index 1: \(item)")
```

How It Works

To get a particular element at a specific index of a tuple, we may use its index.

```
Item at index 1: two
```

8-38. Get tuple element by pattern matching

Problem

I want to get a specific tuple element by matching against a given pattern.

Solution

First, we initialize a test tuple.

```
let tuple = ("one", "two", "three")
```

We want the item at index: 1 (the second element) so that we can safely ignore everything else.

```
let (_, item, _) = tuple
```

Let's see...

```
print("Item at index 1: \(item)")
```

How It Works

To get a particular element at a specific location within a tuple, we may reassign it to another variable and only get the part we want.

```
Item at index 1: two
```

8-39. Insert item at array index

Problem

I want to insert an element at a specific array index.

Solution

First, we initialize a test array.

```
var arr = ["one", "two", "three"]
```

Then we insert our new item at index: 1 (after "one" and before "two").

```
arr.insert("new", at: 1)
```

Let's see our new array...

```
print("Array: \(arr)")
```

How It Works

To insert a particular item at some specific index in an existing array, we may use the Array's insert(_,at:) method.

```
Array: ["one", "new", "two", "three"]
```

8-40. Join array items using separator

Problem

I want to join the elements of a string array, using a specific separator.

Solution

First, we initialize our test array.

```
let arr = [
    "bananas",
    "apples",
    "apricots",
```

```
    "pineapples",
    "oranges"
]
```

Let's join them into a string, using a comma as a separator.

```
let fruit = arr.joined(separator: ",")
```

Let's see...

```
print(fruit)
```

How It Works

In order to join an array's items into a string, we can use the Array's joined(separator:) method.

bananas,apples,apricots,pineapples,oranges

8-41. Loop through an array in reverse

Problem

I want to loop through an array's element in reverse.

Solution

Let's initialize our array, with some values.

```
let arr = ["one", "two", "three"]
```

Iterate through the array.

```
for element in arr.reversed() {
    print(element)
}
```

How It Works

In order to loop through an array in reverse, we can use a *for-in* statement along with our array... reversed, using the Array's reversed method.

```
three
two
one
```

8-42. Loop through an array with index

Problem

I want to loop through an array's elements and keep track of the element's index at the same time.

Solution

Let's initialize our array, with some values.

```
let arr = ["one", "two", "three"]
```

Iterate through the array, while keeping the items' index: Use .enumerated() to convert your array to iterable key-value pairs.

```
for (index,element) in arr.enumerated() {
    print("Item at \(index): \(element)")
}
```

How It Works

In order to loop through an array with its index, we can use a *for-in* statement along with our array... enumerated, that is: using the Array's enumerated method, which will assign an index, to each one of our array's elements.

```
Item at 0: one
Item at 1: two
Item at 2: three
```

8-43. Loop through an array

Problem

I want to loop through an array's elements.

Solution

Let's initialize our array, with some values.

```
let arr = ["one", "two", "three"]
```

Iterate through the array.

```
for element in arr {
    print(element)
}
```

How It Works

In order to loop through an array, we can use a *for-in* statement.

```
one
two
three
```

8-44. Map array values using function

Problem

I want to map an array's values to a new array using a specific function.

Solution

First, we initialize our test array.

```
let numbers = [1, 2, 3, 4, 5, 6, 7, 8, 9, 10]
```

Now, let's say we want the squares of the above numbers. That is: to map each of the above numbers to its squares.

```
let squares = numbers.map { $0 * $0 }
```

And... print the result.

```
print("Our numbers: \(numbers)")
print("Squared: \(squares)")
```

How It Works

If we have an array and want to map its values to new ones, using a specific function, then we can use the Array's map method along with the appropriate closure.

```
Our numbers: [1, 2, 3, 4, 5, 6, 7, 8, 9, 10]
Squared: [1, 4, 9, 16, 25, 36, 49, 64, 81, 100]
```

8-45. Pop last item from array

Problem

I want to retrieve the last element from an array, and remove it from that array.

Solution

First, we set some initial value.

```
var arr = ["one", "two", "three", "four", "five"]
```

Let's pop the last element.

```
let lastElement = arr.removeLast()
```

Let's see...

```
print("Popped element: \(lastElement)")
print("Resulting array: \(arr)")
```

How It Works

In order to pop an array's last element, we can use the Array's removeLast method.

```
Popped element: five
Resulting array: ["one", "two", "three", "four"]
```

8-46. Prepend item to array

Problem

I want to add an element at the beginning of a given array.

Solution

First, we initialize our array.

```
var fruit = ["banana", "apple", "mango", "apricot"]
```

Then, we prepend our new item. That is: Insert it at index 0.

```
fruit.insert("pineapple", at: 0)
```

Let's see our new array...

```
print("Result: \(fruit)")
```

How It Works

Prepending an item to an existing array can be done, using the Array's insert method.

```
Result: ["pineapple", "banana", "apple", "mango", "apricot"]
```

8-47. Reduce array to a single value

Problem

I want to "reduce" an array of numbers to a single value.

Solution

Let's initialize our example array.

```
let numbers = [1, 2, 3, 4, 5, 6]
```

What we want to do is basically add up all the elements. So, we set an initial value, followed by the closure that describes the action to be performed on our array.

Tip: Reduce starts with an initial value, performs some action to this value and the first value it encounters in our array, and then proceeds recursively using the result. And so on... until there are no more elements in our array...

```
let result = numbers.reduce(0, { $0 + $1 })
```

Let's see the result...

```
print("Result: \(result)")
```

How It Works

If we want to combine all elements in an array and reduce it to a single value, we can use the Array's reduce method.

```
Result: 21
```

8-48. Remove all items from array

Problem

I want to remove all elements from a given array.

Solution

First, we initialize a test array.

```
var arr = ["one", "two", "three"]
```

Then we remove all of its contents.

```
arr.removeAll()
```

Let's see our new - empty – array...

```
print("Array: \(arr)")
```

How It Works

To remove all values from an existing array (basically, to empty it), we may use the Array's removeAll method.

```
Array: []
```

8-49. Remove array item by index
Problem

I want to remove a specific element from a given array, by its index.

Solution

First, we initialize a test array.

```
var arr = ["one", "two", "three"]
```

Then we remove the item at index: 1.

```
arr.remove(at: 1)
```

Let's see our new array...

```
print("Array: \(arr)")
```

How It Works

To remove a particular item at some specific index in an existing array, we may use the Array's remove(at:) method.

```
Array: ["one", "three"]
```

8-50. Remove array item by value

Problem

I want to remove a specific element from a given array, by its value.

Solution

First, we initialize a test array.

```
var arr = ["one", "two", "three"]
```

Then, we remove all "two" values.

```
arr = arr.filter { $0 != "two" }
```

Let's see our new array...

```
print("Array: \(arr)")
```

How It Works

To remove a particular value in an existing array, we may use the Array's `filter` method.

```
Array: ["one", "three"]
```

8-51. Remove duplicates from array

Problem

I want to remove all duplicate elements from a given array.

Solution

First, we initialize a test array.

```
var initial = [6, 3, 1, 2, 4, 1, 2, 3, 6, 5, 1, 2]
```

Then, we remove any duplicates.

```
var unique = Array(Set(initial))
```

Let's print our new no-duplicates array.

```
print("Before: \(initial)")
print("Unique: \(unique)")
```

How It Works

To remove all duplicates from a given array, pretty much like PHP'S array_unique, we may use a simple trick: convert the array to a set (by definition they contain unique elements) and then back to an array.

```
Before: [6, 3, 1, 2, 4, 1, 2, 3, 6, 5, 1, 2]
Unique: [6, 5, 2, 3, 1, 4]
```

8-52. Reverse an array

Problem

I want to reverse an array's elements.

Solution

First, we set some initial value.

```
let arr = ["one", "two", "three", "four", "five"]
```

Time to reverse it.

```
let reversed = Array(arr.reversed())
```

Let's see...

```
print("\(arr) => \(reversed)")
```

How It Works

In order to reverse an array, we can use the Array's reversed method.

```
["one", "two", "three", "four", "five"] => ["five", "four",
"three", "two", "one"]
```

8-53. Set array element at index

Problem

I want to set an element's value at a specific index of a given array.

Solution

First, we initialize a test array.

```
var arr = ["one", "two", "three"]
```

We want the set the item at index: 1.

```
arr[1] = "<new>"
```

Let's see...

```
print("Array: \(arr)")
```

How It Works

To assign a particular element at a specific index of an array some new value, we may use its *subscript*.

```
Array: ["one", "<new>", "three"]
```

8-54. Shift first item from array

Problem

I want to retrieve and "shift" the first element of a given array.

Solution

First, we set some initial value.

```
var arr = ["one", "two", "three", "four", "five"]
```

Let's shift the first element.

```
let firstElement = arr.removeFirst()
```

Let's see...

```
print("First element: \(firstElement)")
print("Resulting array: \(arr)")
```

How It Works

In order to shift/pop an array's first element, we can use the Array's removeFirst method.

```
First element: one
Resulting array: ["two", "three", "four", "five"]
```

8-55. Shuffle an array

Problem

I want to – randomly – shuffle an array's elements.

Solution

Note   For an even more efficient implementation, if needed, it would be advisable to have a look into the Fischer-Yates algorithm.

```
import Foundation
```

First, we initialize a test array.

```
var initial = [1, 2, 3, 4, 5, 6]
```

Then we shuffle it.

```
var shuffled = initial.sorted { _,_ in Int.random(in: 0..<1000)
< Int.random(in: 0..<1000) }
```

Let's print our new no-duplicates array.

```
print("Before: \(initial)")
print("Shuffled: \(shuffled)")
```

How It Works

To shuffle an array, aka randomize the order of its elements, we'll be using the arc4random function.

```
Before: [1, 2, 3, 4, 5, 6]
Shuffled: [5, 2, 3, 4, 1, 6]
```

8-56. Sort array of dictionaries by field in ascending order

Problem

I want to sort a given array of dictionaries, by some specific dictionary field, in ascending order.

Solution

First, we initialize a test array.

```
var members = [
    ["name": "John",        "age": 30],
    ["name": "Jane",        "age": 39],
    ["name": "Angela",       "age": 18],
    ["name": "Nick",        "age": 59]
]
```

Now let's say we want to sort our members list, by age.

Note   Given our initial array is of type [String:Any], we'll have to use as! Int in order to force the particular type we need to sort by. Otherwise, the compiler will complain.

```
var sorted = members.sorted { ($0["age"] as! Int) < ($1["age"] as! Int) }
```

Let's print our sorted array...

```
print("Sorted: \(sorted)")
```

179

How It Works

To sort an array containing dictionaries, by dictionary field, in ascending order, we may use the Array's `sorted` method, along with the appropriate closure.

```
Sorted: [["name": "Angela", "age": 18], ["name": "John", "age":
30], ["name": "Jane", "age": 39], ["name": "Nick", "age": 59]]
```

8-57. Sort array of dictionaries by field in descending order

Problem

I want to sort a given array of dictionaries, by some specific dictionary field, in descending order.

Solution

First, we initialize a test array.

```
var members = [
     ["name": "John",      "age": 30],
     ["name": "Jane",      "age": 39],
     ["name": "Angela",    "age": 18],
     ["name": "Nick",      "age": 59]
]
```

Now let's say we want to sort our members list, by age.

Note   Given our initial array is of type [`String:Any`], we'll have to use `as!` `Int` in order to force the particular type we need to sort by. Otherwise, the compiler will complain.

```
var sorted = members.sorted { ($0["age"] as! Int) > ($1["age"]
as! Int) }
```

Let's print our sorted array...

```
print("Sorted: \(sorted)")
```

How It Works

To sort an array containing dictionaries, by dictionary field, in descending order, we may use the Array's sorted method, along with the appropriate closure.

```
Sorted: [["name": "Nick", "age": 59], ["name": "Jane", "age":
39], ["name": "John", "age": 30], ["name": "Angela", "age": 18]]
```

8-58. Sort array of numbers in ascending order

Problem

I want to sort a given array of numbers, in ascending order.

Solution

First, we initialize a test array.

```
var initial = [6, 3, 1, 2, 4]
```

Then we sort the array and get the resulting array.

```
var sorted = initial.sorted()
```

Let's print our sorted array...

```
print("Before: \(initial)")
print("Sorted: \(sorted)")
```

How It Works

To sort an array containing numeric values, in ascending order, that is: from smallest to largest, we may use the Array's `sorted` method.

```
Before: [6, 3, 1, 2, 4]
Sorted: [1, 2, 3, 4, 6]
```

8-59. Sort array of numbers in descending order

Problem

I want to sort a given array of numbers in descending order.

Solution

First, we initialize a test array.

```
var initial = [6, 3, 1, 2, 4]
```

Then, we sort the array and get the resulting array.

```
var sorted = initial.sorted(by: >)
```

Let's print our sorted array...

```
print("Before: \(initial)")
print("Sorted: \(sorted)")
```

How It Works

To sort an array containing numeric values, in descending order, that is: from largest to smallest, we may use the Array's `sorted` method.

```
Before: [6, 3, 1, 2, 4]
Sorted: [6, 4, 3, 2, 1]
```

8-60. Sort array of strings in ascending order

Problem

I want to sort a given array of strings, lexicographically, in ascending order.

Solution

First, we initialize a test array.

```
var initial = ["one", "two", "three", "four", "five", "six"]
```

Then, we sort the array and get the resulting array.

```
var sorted = initial.sorted()
```

Let's print our sorted array...

```
print("Before: \(initial)")
print("Sorted: \(sorted)")
```

How It Works

To sort an array containing string values, in ascending lexicographic order, that is: from the one that'd come first in a dictionary to that which would come last, we may use the Array's sorted method, pretty much as we'd do for a number array.

```
Before: ["one", "two", "three", "four", "five", "six"]
Sorted: ["five", "four", "one", "six", "three", "two"]
```

8-61. Sort array of strings in descending order

Problem

I want to sort a given array of strings, lexicographically, in descending order.

Solution

First, we initialize a test array.

```
var initial = ["one", "two", "three", "four", "five", "six"]
```

Then, we sort the array and get the resulting array.

```
var sorted = initial.sorted(by: >)
```

Let's print our sorted array...

```
print("Before: \(initial)")
print("Sorted: \(sorted)")
```

How It Works

To sort an array containing string values, in descending lexicographic order, that is: from the one that'd come last in a dictionary to that which would come first, we may use the Array's `sorted` method, pretty much as we'd do for a number array.

```
Before: ["one", "two", "three", "four", "five", "six"]
Sorted: ["two", "three", "six", "one", "four", "five"]
```

8-62. Swap items in array by index

Problem

I want to swap two elements in a given array, specifying their indices.

Solution

First, we initialize a test array.

```
var arr = ["zero", "one", "two", "three", "four", "five"]
```

Then we `swapAt` the elements at indices 2 and 3 – meaning: "two" and "three."

```
arr.swapAt(2, 3)
```

Let's see our new rearranged array, "three" will appear before "two" now.

```
print("Array: \(arr)")
```

How It Works

To swap two elements in an existing array by their indices, we can use the swapAt function with references to the individual elements we want to swap.

```
Array: ["zero", "one", "three", "two", "four", "five"]
```

8-63. Write a list comprehension

Problem

I want to write a list comprehension.

Solution

Let's take this set for example:

$E = \{x*x \mid x \text{ in } \{0 \ldots 10\} \text{ and } x \text{ even}\}.$

That is: get a list for all the x's squared (with x between 0 and 10) where x is even.

Let's describe our list of evens – squared.

```
let evenSquared = (0...10).filter { $0 % 2 == 0}
                                 .map    { $0 * $0 }
```

And let's print our list...

```
print("Result: \(evenSquared)")
```

How It Works

List Comprehension is nothing but a fancy way of describing the very natural, easy way that a mathematician usually uses to describe a list.

```
Result: [0, 4, 16, 36, 64, 100]
```

8-64. Write a lazy list comprehension

Problem

I want to write a "lazy" list comprehension.

Solution

Let's take this set for example:

E = {x*x | x in {0 ... 10} and x even}.

That is: get a list for all the x's squared (with x between 0 and 10) where x is even.

However, if we want to do it in pure... functional styling, we'll have to use lazy evaluation.

Let's describe our list of evens – squared.

```
let evenSquared = (0...10).lazy.filter { $0 % 2 == 0}
                                     .map    { $0 * $0 }
```

It's lazy – so, nothing has been calculated so far.

Let's make it calculate our result.

```
let result = Array(evenSquared)
```

Finally, let's print our list...

```
print("Result: \(result)")
```

How It Works

List Comprehensions is nothing but a fancy way of describing the very natural, easy way that a mathematician usually uses to describe a list. And lazy evaluation, or *call-by-need*, is nothing but a strategy that delays the evaluation of an expression until its value is needed.

```
Result: [0, 4, 16, 36, 64, 100]
```

8-65. Check if set contains item
Problem

I want to check if a given set contains a specific element.

Solution

First, we initialize our example set with some values.

```
let fruit : Set = ["banana", "apple", "orange", "pineapple"]
```

Now, let's see...

```
if fruit.contains("banana") {
    print("Yes, our set contains bananas!")
} else {
    print("Nope, no bananas left! :(")
}
```

How It Works

To check if a set contains a particular element, we can use its `contains` method.

```
Yes, our set contains bananas!
```

8-66. Check if set is empty
Problem

I want to check if a given set is empty.

Solution

First, we initialize our example set with some values from an array.

```
let a : Set = [1,2,3]
```

Now, let's see...

```
if a.isEmpty {
    print("Our set is empty :(")
} else {
    print("Of course it's not empty - we just created it!")
}
```

How It Works

To check if a set is empty, we can use its isEmpty property.

```
Of course it's not empty - we just created it!
```

8-67. Check if set is strict subset of another set

Problem

I want to check if a given set is a strict subset of another set.

Solution

First, let's initialize our test sets.

```
let animals : Set = ["dog", "cat", "eagle", "salmon", "mosquito"]
let mammals : Set = ["dog", "cat"]
```

Let's see if mammals is a strict subset of animals.

```
if mammals.isStrictSubset(of: animals) {
    print("Yep, mammals are a strict subset of animals.")
}
```

How It Works

To check if a particular set is a *strict subset* of another set, that is: if all of our set's elements of are contained in another set or sequence, but the two sets are not equal, we can use the Set's isStrictSubset(of:) method.

```
Yep, mammals are a strict subset of animals.
```

8-68. Check if set is strict superset of another set

Problem

I want to check if a given set is a strict superset of another set.

Solution

First, let's initialize our test sets.

```
let animals : Set = ["dog", "cat", "eagle", "salmon", "mosquito"]
let mammals : Set = ["dog", "cat"]
```

Let's see if animals is a strict superset of mammals.

```
if animals.isStrictSuperset(of: mammals) {
    print("Yep, animals are a strict superset of mammals.")
}
```

How It Works

To check if a particular set is a *strict superset* of another set, that is: if our set contains all the elements of another set or sequence, but the two sets are not equal, we can use the Set's isStrictSuperset(of:) method.

```
Yep, animals are a strict superset of mammals.
```

8-69. Check if set is subset of another set

Problem

I want to check if a given set is a subset of another set.

Solution

First, let's initialize our test sets.

```
let animals : Set = ["dog", "cat", "eagle", "salmon", "mosquito"]
let mammals : Set = ["dog", "cat"]
```

Let's see if mammals is a subset of animals.

```
if mammals.isSubset(of: animals) {
    print("Yep, mammals are a subset of animals.")
}
```

How It Works

To check if a particular set is a *subset* of another set, that is: if all of our set's elements of are contained in another set or sequence, we can use the Set's isSubset(of:) method.

```
Yep, mammals are a subset of animals.
```

8-70. Check if set is superset of another set

Problem

I want to check if a given set is a superset of another set.

Solution

First, let's initialize our test sets.

```
let animals : Set = ["dog", "cat", "eagle", "salmon", "mosquito"]
let mammals : Set = ["dog", "cat"]
```

Let's see if animals is a superset of mammals.

```
if animals.isSuperset(of: mammals) {
    print("Yep, animals are a superset of mammals.")
}
```

How It Works

To check if a particular set is a *superset* of another set, that is: if our set contains all the elements of another set or sequence, we can use the Set's isSuperset(of:) method.

```
Yep, animals are a superset of mammals.
```

8-71. Check if two sets are equal

Problem

I want to check if two different sets are equal.

Solution

First, we initialize our sets from arrays.

```
let a : Set = [1,2,3]
let b : Set = [4,5,6]
```

Let's see...

```
if a == b {
    print("Yep, the sets are equal")
} else {
    print("Nope, they are different sets")
}
```

How It Works

To compare two sets and check if they are equal, we can use the == comparison operator.

```
Nope, they are different sets
```

8-72. Check if two sets have common items

Problem

I want to check if two different sets have common elements.

Solution

First, we initialize our example sets with some values.

```
let reptiles : Set = ["chameleon", "snake", "lizard"]
let birds : Set = ["eagle", "crow", "seagull"]
```

Now, let's see if these two have any elements in common.

```
if reptiles.isDisjoint(with: birds) {
    print("Well, quite obviously, they have no members in
    common.")
} else {
    print("Yep, there are some common elements - wait, what?!")
}
```

How It Works

To check if two sets have elements in common, we can the Set's isDisjoint(with:) method.

```
Well, quite obviously, they have no members in common.
```

8-73. Create an empty set

Problem

I want to create an empty Set object.

Solution

First approach: Just declare the type and set to an empty array.

```
var a : Set<String> = []
```

Second approach: Use a Set constructor.

```
let b = Set<String>()
```

Let's print our empty sets...

```
print("a: \(a), b: \(b)")
```

How It Works

In order to create an empty set, the only thing you have to specify is the type of items it's going to contain. That is String, Int, or... anything.

```
a: [], b: []
```

8-74. Create NSSet from Set
Problem

I want to create an NSSet object from a given set.

Solution

```
import Foundation
```

First, we initialize our example set.

```
let a : Set = ["one", "two", "three"]
```

Let's convert it to an NSSet.

```
let b = NSSet(set: a)
```

Let's try using the NSSet's 'hash' property (not available for Swift pure sets) to make sure we made it.

```
print("Final set's hash: \(b.hash)")
print("Yep, it's an NSSet!")
```

How It Works

In order to convert/bridge a Set to an NSSet, for example, when you need to access APIs that expect data in an NSSet instance, or need to use some NSSet-specific methods, we can use the NSSet(set:) initializer.

```
Final set's hash: 3
Yep, it's an NSSet!
```

8-75. Find the difference of two sets

Problem

I want to find the difference of two different sets.

Solution

First, let's initialize our test sets.

```
let first : Set = [1, 2, 3, 4]
let second : Set = [3, 4, 5, 6]
```

Let's find the difference.

```
let result = first.subtracting(second)
```

...and print the resulting set.

```
print("Result: \(result)")
```

How It Works

To find the difference of two sets, that is: the set that contains the elements of set A, after subtracting the elements of set B, we can use the Set's subtracting method.

```
Result: [2, 1]
```

8-76. Find the intersection of two sets

Problem

I want to find the intersection of two different sets.

Solution

First, let's initialize our test sets.

```
let first : Set = [1, 2, 3, 4]
let second : Set = [3, 4, 5, 6]
```

Let's find the intersection.

```
let result = first.intersection(second)
```

...and print the resulting set.

```
print("Result: \(result)")
```

How It Works

To find the intersection of two sets, that is: the set that contains only the common elements of the two sets, we can use the Set's `intersection` method.

```
Result: [3, 4]
```

8-77. Find the symmetric difference of two sets

Problem

I want to find the symmetric difference of two different sets.

Solution

First, let's initialize our test sets.

```
let first : Set = [1, 2, 3, 4]
let second : Set = [3, 4, 5, 6]
```

Let's find the symmetric difference.

```
let result = first.symmetricDifference(second)
```

...and print the resulting set.

```
print("Result: \(result)")
```

How It Works

To find the symmetric difference of two sets, that is: the set that contains the elements in one of the two sets, but not in both of them, we can use the Set's symmetricDifference method.

```
Result: [5, 6, 2, 1]
```

8-78. Find the union of two sets

Problem

I want to find the union of two different sets.

Solution

First, let's initialize our test sets.

```
let first : Set = [1, 2, 3, 4]
let second : Set = [3, 4, 5, 6]
```

Let's find the union.

```
let result = first.union(second)
```

...and print the resulting set.

```
print("Result: \(result)")
```

How It Works

To find the union of two sets, that is: the set that contains the elements of both sets, we can use the Set's union method.

```
Result: [5, 6, 2, 3, 1, 4]
```

8-79. Get size of set

Problem

I want to get the size of a given set.

Solution

First, we initialize our example set with some values from an array.

```
let a : Set = [1,2,3]
```

Now, let's count how many items we've got...

```
print("The set contains \(a.count) elements")
```

How It Works

To check the size of a Set, we can use its count property.

```
The set contains 3 elements
```

8-80. Loop through a set

Problem

I want to loop through a given set's elements.

Solution

Let's initialize our Set with some values from an array literal.

```
let mySet : Set = ["one", "two", "three"]
```

Iterate through the set elements.

```
for element in mySet {
    print(element)
}
```

How It Works

In order to loop through a set, we can use a *for-in* statement.

```
one
three
two
```

8-81. Remove all items from set

Problem

I want to remove all elements from a given set.

Solution

First, we initialize a test set.

```
var basket : Set = ["steak", "oranges", "milk"]
```

Then we remove all of its contents.

```
basket.removeAll()
```

Let's see our new - empty - set.

```
print("Basket: \(basket)")
```

How It Works

To remove all values from an existing set (basically, to empty it), we may use the Set's removeAll method.

```
Basket: []
```

8-82. Summary

In this chapter, we learned how we can efficiently manipulate and play with our arrays and sets.

In the next chapter, we'll be looking into one more of the most used objects in Swift: Dictionaries.

CHAPTER 9

Dictionaries

In programming, a dictionary is a general-purpose data structure, used to store a group of objects, in a "real" dictionary-like lemma-definition approach - or as group of key-value pairs, properly put.

In this chapter, we'll explore most of Swift's dictionary-related capabilities and learn how to create new ones, add/remove keys, merge them, and move on to even more advanced topics, such as handling property lists.

9-1. Add key-value pair to dictionary
Problem

I want to add a key-value pair to an existing dictionary

Solution

Let's initialize our test dictionary.

```
var user = [
    "name"       : "John",
    "surname"    : "Doe",
    "email"      : "info@iswift.org"
]
```

OK, let's add some more info.

```
user["nationality"] = "US"
```

And print the result...

```
print("User: \(user)")
```

How It Works

A dictionary is a collection of key-value pairs. In order to add another key with a value, we can do it pretty much like changing an already existing key, that is: by using the subscript along with the value's key and assign it the desired value.

```
User: ["name": "John", "surname": "Doe", "email": "info@iswift.
org", "nationality": "US"]
```

9-2. Check if dictionary is empty

Problem

I want to check if a dictionary is empty.

Solution

First, we initialize our example dictionary with some data.

```
let a = [
    "name"       : "John",
    "surname"    : "Doe"
]
```

Now, let's see...

```
if a.isEmpty {
    print("Our dictionary is empty :(")
} else {
    print("Of course it's not empty - we just created it!")
}
```

How It Works

To check if a dictionary is empty, we can use its isEmpty property.

```
Of course it's not empty - we just created it!
```

9-3. Check if key exists in dictionary
Problem

I want to check if a specific key exists in a given dictionary.

Solution

First, we initialize our example dictionary.

```
var d = [
    "name"      :     "John",
    "surname"   :     "Doe",
    "email"     :      "info@iswift.org"
]
```

Now, let's see...

```
if d["address"] != nil {
    print("Yes, address found!")
} else {
    print("Ooops, no address found!")
}
```

How It Works

To check if a given dictionary contains a specific key, we may use the dictionary's *subscript*.

```
Ooops, no address found!
```

9-4. Check if object is dictionary
Problem

I want to check if a given object is of type dictionary.

Solution

First, we initialize our example "object" – let's make it a dictionary, as expected.

```
var a : Any = [
    "name"       :     "John",
    "surname"    :     "Doe"
]
```

Now, let's see...

```
if a is [String:String] {
    print("Yes, it's a String:String dictionary. Well done!")
} else {
    print("Oh, no, this is not a dictionary!")
}
```

How It Works

To check if an object is of type dictionary, we can use an `X is a dictionary` or `X is [type:type]` statement.

```
Yes, it's a String:String dictionary. Well done!
```

9-5. Check if two dictionaries are equal

Problem

I want to check if two different dictionaries are equal.

Solution

First, we initialize our dictionaries.

```
let a = ["name": "John", "surname": "Doe"]
let b = ["name": "Jane", "surname": "Doe"]
```

Let's see...

```
if a == b {
    print("Yep, the dictionaries are equal")
} else {
    print("Nope, they are different dictionaries")
}
```

How It Works

To compare two dictionaries and check if they are equal, we can use the ==
comparison operator.

```
Nope, they are different dictionaries
```

9-6. Convert dictionary to array of tuples
Problem

I want to convert a given dictionary to an array of key-value tuples.

Solution

First, we initialize an example dictionary.

```
let fruit = [
    "banana"     : "yellow",
    "apple"      : "red",
    "watermelon" : "green"
]
```

Let's map it to an array of tuples.

```
let fruitArray = fruit.map { ($0,$1) }
```

And... print the result.

```
print("Fruit: \(fruitArray)")
```

How It Works

If we have a dictionary, we can convert it into an array, by mapping its key-value pairs to tuples using the dictionary's map method.

```
Fruit: [("watermelon", "green"), ("apple", "red"), ("banana",
"yellow")]
```

9-7. Convert dictionary to JSON string

Problem

I want to convert a dictionary object to its corresponding JSON string representation.

Solution

```
import Foundation
```

First, let's create an example dictionary.

```
let dict : [String:Any] = [
    "name"        : "John",
    "surname"     : "Doe",
    "age"         : 69
]
do {

    // Convert our dictionary to Json data

    let json = try JSONSerialization.data(withJSONObject:
    dict, options: .prettyPrinted)
```

```
    // Convert our Json data to string

    let str = String(data: json, encoding: .utf8)

    // And if all went well, print it out

    print(str ?? "Ooops... Error converting Json to string!")
}
catch let error
{
    print("Error: \(error)")
}
```

How It Works

In order to convert a Swift dictionary to JSON, we may use the
JSONSerialization class.

```
{
  "name" : "John",
  "surname" : "Doe",
  "age" : 69
}
```

9-8. Convert JSON string to dictionary

Problem

I want to convert an object represented as a JSON string to a dictionary
object.

Solution

```
import Foundation
```

First, let's set some test JSON.

```
let json = "{\"name\": \"John\", \"surname\": \"Doe\",
\"age\": 69 }"
```

Then, we convert it to a Data object.

```
if let data = json.data(using: .utf8) {

    // if everything went fine,
    // it's time to convert our Data object to a Dictionary

    let result = try? JSONSerialization.jsonObject(with:
    data, options: []) as! [String:Any]

    // And finally, what about printing out our dictionary?

    print(result ?? "Ooops... Error converting Json!")

}
```

How It Works

In order to convert a JSON string to a Swift dictionary, we may use the
JSONSerialization class.

```
["name": John, "surname": Doe, "age": 69]
```

9-9. Create a dictionary with literal

Problem

I want to create a dictionary object from a dictionary literal.

Solution

This is a dictionary, with its type automatically inferred.

```
let a = [
    "Country"   : "Spain",
    "Capital"   : "Madrid"
]
```

This is the same one, but this time let's set a type, for example, keys of String type, with values of String type.

```
let b : [String:String] = [
    "Country"   : "Spain",
    "Capital"   : "Madrid"
]
```

Let's create a mixed dictionary with different types of elements. And different types of keys. This is rather tricky.

This time we have to explicitly say it's of type [AnyHashable:Any]. Otherwise, the compiler will complain.

```
let c : [AnyHashable:Any] = [
    1           : "one",
    "two"       : 2
]
```

Let's see what we've managed...

```
print("a: \(a)")
print("b: \(b)")
print("c: \(c)")
```

How It Works

Creating a dictionary from a dictionary literal is as simple as listing your key-value pairs (with a : between the two), separated by commas, surrounded by a pair of square brackets.

```
a: ["Capital": "Madrid", "Country": "Spain"]
b: ["Capital": "Madrid", "Country": "Spain"]
c: [AnyHashable(1): "one", AnyHashable("two"): 2]
```

9-10. Create an empty dictionary
Problem

I want to create an empty dictionary object.

Solution

First approach: Use the [:] empty dictionary expression.

```
let a : [String:String] = [:]
```

Second approach: Use a dictionary constructor.

```
let b = [String:Any]()
```

Third approach: "Enforce" its type with as.

```
let c = [:] as [String:Int]
```

Let's print our three... empty dictionaries.

```
print("a: \(a), b: \(b), c: \(c)")
```

How It Works

In order to create an empty dictionary, it works pretty much as with the arrays; the only thing you have to specify is the type of items (keys and values) it's going to contain.

```
a: [:], b: [:], c: [:]
```

9-11. Create NSDictionary from dictionary
Problem

I want to create an NSDictionary object from a dictionary.

Solution

```
import Foundation
```

First, we initialize our example array with some values.

```
let dict = [
    "name"      : "John",
    "surname"   : "Doe",
    "email"     : "info@iswift.org"
]
```

Let's convert it to an NSDictionary.

```
let b = NSDictionary(dictionary: dict)
```

Let's try using the NSDictionary's hash property (not available for Swift pure dictionaries) to make sure we made it.

```
print("Final dictionary's hash: \(b.hash)")
print("Yep, it's an NSDictionary!")
```

How It Works

In order to convert/bridge a dictionary to an NSDictionary, for example, when you need to access APIs that expect data in an NSDictionary instance, we can use the NSDictionary(dictionary:) initializer.

```
Final dictionary's hash: 3
Yep, it's an NSDictionary!
```

9-12. Get array of keys in dictionary
Problem

I want to get a given dictionary's keys as an array.

Solution

Let's initialize our test dictionary.

```
let dict = [
    "name"      : "John",
    "surname"   : "Doe",
    "email"     : "info@iswift.org"
]
```

Then, we get its keys into an array.

```
let keys = Array(dict.keys)
```

Let's print the result...

```
print("Our dictionary keys: \(keys)")
```

How It Works

A dictionary is a collection of *key-value* pairs. But what if we want to get just the keys? For that, we can use the dictionary's keys property.

```
Our dictionary keys: ["name", "surname", "email"]
```

9-13. Get dictionary value for key

Problem

I want to get the value of a specific key from a given dictionary.

Solution

Let's initialize our test dictionary.

```
let user = [
    "name"      : "John",
    "surname"   : "Doe",
    "email"     : "info@iswift.org"
]
```

Then, we get the user's name.

Careful: This is optional; and it is not guaranteed that we'll find this particular key in the dictionary.

```
if let userName = user["name"] {

    // Let's print the result

    print("Our user's name is: \(userName)")

}
```

How It Works

A dictionary is a collection of key-value pairs. In order to retrieve a specific value, we may use the *subscript* along with the value's key.

```
Our user's name is: John
```

9-14. Get size of dictionary
Problem

I want to get the size of a given dictionary.

Solution

First, we initialize our example dictionary with some date.

```
let a = [
    "name"      : "John",
    "surname"   : "Doe",
    "email"     : "info@iswift.org"
]
```

Now, let's count how many key-value pairs we've got...

```
print("The dictionary contains \(a.count) elements")
```

How It Works

To check the size of a dictionary, we can use its `count` property.

```
The dictionary contains 3 elements
```

9-15. Loop through a Dictionary

Problem

I want to loop through a dictionary, keeping track of each key-value pair.

Solution

Let's initialize our example dictionary.

```
let userInfo = [
     "name"     : "John",
     "surname"  : "Doe",
     "email"    : "info@iswift.org"
]
```

Let's iterate through our dictionary...

```
for (item,value) in userInfo {
     print("\(item) = \(value)")
}
```

How It Works

Looping through a dictionary is just as easy as looping through an array. Only we have to keep track of both parts of each pair: key and value.

```
name = John
surname = Doe
email = info@iswift.org
```

9-16. Merge two dictionaries

Problem

I want to merge two different dictionaries into a new one.

Solution

First, we initialize our example dictionaries.

Note   The dictionary that is going to change must be declared as a variable (in this case, dictB will be merged into dictA).

```
var dictA = [ "1" : "one", "2" : "two", "4" : "four" ]
let dictB = [ "1" : "uno", "3" : "tres" ]
```

Let's loop through our dictB.

```
for (key,value) in dictB {

    // if key doesn't exist, create it
    // if it does exist, update it

    dictA[key] = value
}
```

Now, let's print our new dictionary...

```
print("Merged: \(dictA)")
```

How It Works

If we have two dictionaries and want to merge them, that is: to add one dictionary's items to another one, updating keys if necessary; there is no built-in method, but we can loop and update the keys/values accordingly.

```
Merged: ["3": "tres", "2": "two", "1": "uno", "4": "four"]
```

9-17. Read contents of Plist from file into dictionary

Problem

I want to read the contents of a Property List (Plist) file into a dictionary object.

For example:

```
<?xml version="1.0" encoding="UTF-8"?>
<!DOCTYPE plist PUBLIC "-//Apple//DTD PLIST 1.0//EN"
"http://www.apple.com/DTDs/PropertyList-1.0.dtd">
<plist version="1.0">
<dict>
    <key>Books</key>
    <array>
        <dict>
            <key>author</key>
            <string>Fyodor Dostoyevsky</string>
            <key>title</key>
            <string>Crime and Punishment</string>
        </dict>
        <dict>
```

```
            <key>author</key>
            <string>George Orwell</string>
            <key>title</key>
            <string>Animal Farm</string>
        </dict>
    </array>
</dict>
</plist>
```

Solution

```
import Foundation
```

Now, let's set our Plist path.

```
let path = "tests/test.plist"
```

And read our Plist.

```
if let data = try? Data(contentsOf: URL(fileURLWithPath: path)) {

    var format = PropertyListSerialization.
    PropertyListFormat.xml
    let dict = try? PropertyListSerialization.
    propertyList(from: data, options: [], format: &format)
    as! [String : String]

    // Finally, we print out the result

    print(dict ?? "Error converting Plist")

}
```

How It Works

In order to read a property list (XML Plist) string as a dictionary, we may use PropertyListSerialization's propertyList method.

9-18. Read contents of Plist from string into dictionary

Problem

I want to read the contents of a Property List (Plist) string into a dictionary object.

Solution

```
import Foundation
```

First, we initialize our Plist string.

```
let plist = "<?xml version=\"1.0\" encoding=\"UTF-8\"?>" +
"<!DOCTYPE plist PUBLIC \"-//Apple//DTD PLIST 1.0//EN\"
\"http://www.apple.com/DTDs/PropertyList-1.0.dtd\">" +
"<plist version=\"1.0\">" +
    "<dict>" +
        "<key>one</key>" +
        "<string>value</string>" +
        "<key>two</key>" +
        "<string>another value</string>" +
    "</dict>" +
"</plist>"
```

Now, let's read it.

```
let data = plist.data(using: .utf8)
var format = PropertyListSerialization.PropertyListFormat.xml

let dict = try? PropertyListSerialization.propertyList(from:
data!, options: [], format: &format) as! [String : String]
```

And print out the result...

```
print(dict ?? "Error converting plist")
```

How It Works

In order to read a property list (XML Plist) string as a dictionary, we may use PropertyListSerialization's propertyList method.

```
["one": "value", "two": "another value"]
```

9-19. Remove all items from dictionary
Problem

I want to remove all elements from a given dictionary.

Solution

First, we initialize a test dictionary.

```
var user = [
    "name"      : "John",
    "surname"   : "Doe",
    "email"     : "info@iswift.org"
]
```

Then, we remove all of its contents.

```
user.removeAll()
```

Let's see our new - empty – dictionary...

```
print("User: \(user)")
```

How It Works

To remove all values from an existing dictionary (basically: empty it), we may use the dictionary's removeAll method.

```
User: [:]
```

9-20. Remove dictionary item by key

Problem

I want to remove a specific item from a given dictionary, by its key.

Solution

First, we initialize a test dictionary.

```
var user = [
    "name"      : "John",
    "surname"   : "Doe",
    "email"     : "info@iswift.org"
]
```

Then we delete its name or, literally, remove its values with a name key.

```
user.removeValue(forKey: "name")
```

Let's see the resulting dictionary…

```
print("User: \(user)")
```

How It Works

To remove a particular key-value pair from an existing dictionary, we may use the dictionary's removeValue(forKey:) method.

```
User: ["surname": "Doe", "email": "info@iswift.org"]
```

9-21. Set dictionary value by key

Problem

I want to set the value of a specific key in a given dictionary.

Solution

Let's initialize our test dictionary.

```
var user = [
    "name"      : "John",
    "surname"   : "Doe",
    "email"     : "info@iswift.org"
]
```

What about changing the user's name?

```
user["name"] = "Jane"
```

And print the result…

```
print("User: \(user)")
```

How It Works

A dictionary is a collection of *key-value* pairs. In order to set a specific value, we may use the subscript along with the value's key and assign the new value.

```
User: ["name": "Jane", "surname": "Doe", "email": "info@iswift.
org"]
```

9-22. Summary

In this chapter, we learned how we can make use of one of the most powerful constructs in Swift: the dictionary.

In the next chapter, we'll be looking into more advanced Swift topics: from working with numbers and dates, to interacting with the file system, performing web requests, or even launching system processes.

PART III

Advanced

CHAPTER 10

Numbers and Dates

Numbers or numeric values, and dates, are one of the most common things a programmer has to deal with daily.

In this chapter, we'll explore different ways that we can handle numbers in Swift, convert to and from different units, or make use of all of Swift's mathematical capabilities and also see how we can make our life easier when working with date objects.

10-1. Calculate average of elements in array

Problem

I want to calculate the average of all elements in a given number array.

Solution

First, we initialize our example array.

```
let numbers = [1, 2, 3, 4, 5, 6]
```

Then, we calculate the average.

Note   To get the "real" average, we must make sure both parts –
the average and the count – are Double and not integers.

```
let average = Double(numbers.reduce(0, +)) / Double(numbers.count)
```

Let's see the result...

```
print("The average of our array is: \(average)")
```

How It Works

If we want to calculate the average of the elements in a given array, we can
use the Array's reduce method and count property.

```
The average of our array is: 3.5
```

10-2. Calculate median of elements in array

Problem

I want to calculate the median of all the elements in a given number array.

Solution

Let's initialize our example array.

```
let numbers = [5, 1, 3, 2, 4, 6]
```

First, we'll sort our array, from smallest to largest.

```
let sorted = numbers.sorted()
```

Then, we'll take the "middle" value – if there is one (if there is an odd number of elements in our array). Otherwise, we take the average of the two middle values.

```
let median = sorted.count % 2 == 1 ? Double(sorted
[sorted.count/2])
                                                    :
Double(sorted[sorted.count/2-1] + sorted[sorted.count/2]) / 2.0
```

Let's see the result...

```
print("The median of our array is: \(median)")
```

How It Works

If we want to calculate the median of the elements in a given array, we can use the Array's sorted method.

```
The median of our array is: 3.5
```

10-3. Calculate product of elements in array

Problem

I want to calculate the product of all the elements in a given number array.

Solution

First, we initialize our example array.

```
let numbers = [2, 3, 4, 5]
```

Then, we calculate the product.

```
let product = numbers.reduce(1, *)
```

Let's see the result...

```
print("The product of our array's elements is: \(product)")
```

How It Works

If we want to calculate the product of all elements in a given array, we can use the Array's reduce method.

```
The product of our array's elements is: 120
```

10-4. Calculate sum of elements in array
Problem

I want to calculate the sum of all the elements in a given number array.

Solution

First, we initialize our example array.

```
let numbers = [1, 2, 3, 4, 5, 6]
```

Then, we calculate the sum.

```
let sum = numbers.reduce(0, +)
```

Let's see the result...

```
print("The sum of our array's elements is: \(sum)")
```

How It Works

If we want to calculate the sum of all elements in a given array, we can use the Array's reduce method.

```
The sum of our array's elements is: 21
```

10-5. Calculate the base-2 logarithm of a number

Problem

I want to calculate the base-2 logarithm of a given number.

Solution

```
import Foundation
```

First, we set our number.

```
let num = 16.0
```

And calculate its logarithm.

```
let result = _log2(num)
```

Let's see the result...

```
print("Result: \(result)")
```

How It Works

In order to calculate the base-2 logarithm of a number, we may use the _log2 function.

```
Result: 4.0
```

10-6. Calculate the cosine of an angle

Problem

I want to calculate the cosine of a given angle.

Solution

```
import Foundation
```

First, we set our (180-degree) angle and convert it to radians.

```
let angle = 180.0 * Double.pi / 180
```

And calculate its cosine.

```
let cosine = cos(angle)
```

Let's see the result...

```
print("Result: \(cosine)")
```

How It Works

In order to calculate the cosine of an angle, we may use the cos function.

```
Result: -1.0
```

10-7. Calculate the exponential of a number

Problem

I want to calculate the exponential of a given number.

Solution

```
import Foundation
```

First, we set our number.

```
let num = 3.0
```

And calculate its exponential.

```
let result = exp(num)
```

Let's see the result...

```
print("Result: \(result)")
```

How It Works

In order to calculate the exponential of a number, that is: the power $e \wedge x$, we may use the exp function.

```
Result: 20.0855369231877
```

10-8. Calculate the inverse cosine of a number

Problem

I want to calculate the inverse cosine of a given number.

Solution

```
import Foundation
```

First, we set our number.

```
let num = -1.0
```

And calculate its inverse cosine.

```
let inv = acos(num)
```

Lastly, we may also convert it to degrees.

```
let angle = inv * 180 / Double.pi
```

Let's see the result...

```
print("Result: \(angle)")
```

How It Works

In order to calculate the inverse cosine of a number, we may use the acos function.

```
Result: 180.0
```

10-9. Calculate the inverse sine of a number
Problem

I want to calculate the inverse sine of a given number.

Solution

```
import Foundation
```

First, we set our number.

```
let num = 1.0
```

And calculate its inverse sine.

```
let inv = asin(num)
```

Lastly, we may also convert it to degrees.

```
let angle = inv * 180 / Double.pi
```

Let's see the result...

```
print("Result: \(angle)")
```

How It Works

In order to calculate the inverse sine of a number, we may use the `asin` function.

```
Result: 90.0
```

10-10. Calculate the inverse tangent of a number

Problem

I want to calculate the inverse tangent of a given number.

Solution

```
import Foundation
```

First, we set our number.

```
let num = 1.0
```

And calculate its inverse tangent.

```
let inv = atan(num)
```

Lastly, we may also convert it to degrees.

```
let angle = inv * 180 / Double.pi
```

Let's see the result...

```
print("Result: \(angle)")
```

How It Works

In order to calculate the inverse tangent of a number, we may use the atan function.

```
Result: 45.0
```

10-11. Calculate the logarithm of a number

Problem

I want to calculate the logarithm of a given number.

Solution

```
import Foundation
```

First, we set our number.

```
let num = 5.0
```

And calculate its logarithm.

```
let result = _log(num)
```

Let's see the result...

```
print("Result: \(result)")
```

How It Works

In order to calculate the (natural) logarithm of a number, we may use the _log function.

```
Result: 1.6094379124341
```

10-12. Calculate the nth factorial

Problem

I want to calculate the factorial of a given number.

Solution

Let's calculate the 5th factorial (5!) – basically, we take the numbers 1,2,3,4,5 and find their product.

Careful: trying that with a larger number will quickly lead to an overflow!

```
let factorial = (1...5).reduce(1, *)
```

Let's see the result...

```
print("5! = \(factorial)")
```

How It Works

The Nth factorial is basically the product of numbers from *1 up to N*. That's why we can use the array's reduce method along with the appropriate range.

```
5! = 120
```

10-13. Calculate the nth root of a number
Problem

I want to calculate a specific root of a given number.

Solution

```
import Foundation
```

First, we set our number.

```
let num = 16.0
```

And calculate its 4th root.

```
let root = pow(num, 1/4)
```

Let's see the result...

```
print("The 4th root of \(num) is: \(root)")
```

How It Works

In order to calculate the *Nth root* of a number, we may use the pow function.

```
The 4th root of 16.0 is: 2.0
```

10-14. Calculate the power of a number

Problem

I want to calculate the power of a given number.

Solution

```
import Foundation
```

First, we set our number.

```
let num = 5.0
```

And calculate the power (*num ^ 3*).

```
let power = pow(num, 3)
```

Let's see the result...

```
print("\(num) ^ 3 = \(power)")
```

How It Works

In order to calculate the power of a number, we may use the pow function.

```
5.0 ^ 3 = 125.0
```

241

10-15. Calculate the sine of an angle

Problem

I want to calculate the sine of a given angle.

Solution

```
import Foundation
```

First, we set our (90-degree) angle and convert it to radians.

```
let angle = 90.0 * Double.pi / 180
```

And calculate its sine.

```
let sine = sin(angle)
```

Let's see the result...

```
print("Result: \(sine)")
```

How It Works

In order to calculate the sine of an angle, we may use the `sin` function.

```
Result: 1.0
```

10-16. Calculate the square of a number

Problem

I want to calculate the square of a given number.

Solution

```
import Foundation
```

First, we set our number.

```
let num = 3.0
```

And calculate its square.

```
let squared = pow(num, 2)
```

Let's see the result...

```
print("\(num) ^ 2 = \(squared)")
```

How It Works

In order to calculate the square of a number, we may use the pow function.

```
3.0 ^ 2 = 9.0
```

10-17. Calculate the square root of a number

Problem

I want to calculate the square root of a given number.

Solution

```
import Foundation
```

First, we set our number.

```
let num = 16.0
```

And calculate its square root.

```
let root = sqrt(num)
```

Let's see the result...

```
print("The square root of \(num) is: \(root)")
```

How It Works

In order to calculate the square root of a number, we may use the sqrt function.

```
The square root of 16.0 is: 4.0
```

10-18. Calculate the tangent of an angle
Problem

I want to calculate the tangent of a given angle.

Solution

```
import Foundation
```

First, we set our (45-degree) angle and convert it to radians.

```
let angle = 45.0 * Double.pi / 180
```

And calculate its tangent.

```
let tangent = tan(angle)
```

Let's see the result...

```
print("Result: \(tangent)")
```

How It Works

In order to calculate the tangent of an angle, we may use the tan function.

```
Result: 1.0
```

10-19. Check if object is integer
Problem

I want to check if a given object is of type Int.

Solution

First, we initialize our example "object" - let's make it a string.

```
var a : Any = "nope"
```

Now, let's see...

```
if a is Int {
    print("Yes, it's an integer. Yay!")
} else {
    print("Oh, no, something went wrong. it's not an
    integer!")
}
```

How It Works

To check if an object is of type Int, we can use an X is Int statement.

```
Oh, no, something went wrong. it's not an integer!
```

10-20. Convert between angle units

Problem

I want to make a conversion between different angle units.

Solution

Available angle units: .arcMinutes, .arcSeconds, .degrees, .gradians, .radians, .revolutions

```
import Foundation
```

Let's make sure we're on OSX 10.12 or newer. Otherwise, this won't work.

```
if #available(OSX 10.12, *) {

    // First, we set some example value, in degrees

    let angle = Measurement(value: 100, unit: UnitAngle.
    degrees)

    // Then we convert our angle to radians

    let converted = angle.converted(to: .radians)

    // And print it out

    print("\(angle) = \(converted)")
} else {
    print(":-(")
}
```

How It Works

In order to convert a given value between different angle units, that is: from degrees to radians, from gradians to revolutions, and so on, you may use the very handy Measurement class.

```
100.0 ° = 1.74532862792735 rad
```

10-21. Convert between area units
Problem

I want to make a conversion between different area units.

Solution

Available area units:

```
.acres, .ares, .hectares, .squareCentimeters, .squareFeet,
.squareInches, .squareKilometers, .squareMegameters,
.squareMeters, .squareMicrometers, .squareMiles,
.squareMillimeters, .squareNanometers, .squareYards
```

```
import Foundation
```

Let's make sure we're on OSX 10.12 or newer. Otherwise, this won't work.

```
if #available(OSX 10.12, *) {

    // First, we set some example value, in square meters

    let area = Measurement(value: 1000, unit: UnitArea.
    squareMeters)

    // Then we convert our area to acres

    let converted = area.converted(to: .acres)
```

```
    // And print it out

    print("\(area) = \(converted)")

} else {
    print(":-(")
}
```

How It Works

In order to convert a given value between different area units, that is: from square meters to hectares, from acres to square yards, and so on, you may use the very handy Measurement class.

```
1000.0 m² = 0.247105163015276 ac
```

10-22. Convert between length units
Problem

I want to make a conversion between different length units.

Solution

Available length units:

```
.astronomicalUnits, .centimeters, .decameters, .decimeters,
.fathoms, .feet, .furlongs, .hectometers, .inches, .kilometers,
.lightyears, .megameters, .meters, .micrometers, .miles,
.millimeters, .nanometers, .nauticalMiles, .parsecs,
.picometers, .scandinavianMiles, .yards
```

```
import Foundation
```

Let's make sure we're on OSX 10.12 or newer. Otherwise, this won't work.

```
if #available(OSX 10.12, *) {

    // First, we set some example value, in meters

    let length = Measurement(value: 100, unit: UnitLength.
    meters)

    // Then we convert our length to feet

    let converted = length.converted(to: .feet)

    // And print it out

    print("\(length) = \(converted)")
} else {
    print(":-(")
}
```

How It Works

In order to convert a given value between different length units, that is: from meters to feet, from inches to yards, and so on, you may use the very handy Measurement class.

```
100.0 m = 328.083989501312 ft
```

10-23. Convert between volume units
Problem

I want to make a conversion between different volume units.

Solution

Available volume units:

```
.acreFeet, .bushels, .centiliters, .cubicCentimeters,
.cubicDecimeters, .cubicFeet, .cubicInches, .cubicKilometers,
.cubicMeters, .cubicMiles, .cubicMillimeters,
.cubicYards, .cups, .deciliters, .fluidOunces, .gallons,
.imperialFluidOunces, .imperialGallons, .imperialPints,
.imperialQuarts, .imperialTablespoons, .imperialTeaspoons,
.kiloliters, .liters, .megaliters, .metricCups, .milliliters,
.pints, .quarts, .tablespoons, .teaspoons
```

```
import Foundation
```

Let's make sure we're on OSX 10.12 or newer. Otherwise, this won't work.

```
if #available(OSX 10.12, *) {

    // First, we set some example value, in liters

    let volume = Measurement(value: 1, unit: UnitVolume.
    liters)

    // Then we convert our volume to tablespoons

    let converted = volume.converted(to: .tablespoons)

    // And print it out

    print("\(volume) = \(converted)")
} else {
    print(":-(")
}
```

How It Works

In order to convert a given value between different volume units, that is: from square cubic meters to bushels, or even liters to teaspoons, you may use the very handy `Measurement` class.

```
1.0 L = 67.6278843292666 tbsp
```

10-24. Convert degrees to radians

Problem

I want to convert an angle, from degrees to radians.

Solution

```
import Foundation
```

Let's set our test value.

```
let degrees = 21.0
```

Then, we convert it to radians.

```
let radians = degrees * Double.pi / 180.0
```

And print out the result...

```
print("\(degrees) degrees = \(radians) radians")
```

How It Works

In order to convert degrees to radians, we can use the known formula:
```
r = d * pi / 180
```

```
21.0 degrees = 0.366519142918809 radians
```

10-25. Convert double to integer

Problem

I want to convert a given double number to Int.

Solution

Let's create our test number.

```
let d : Double = 18.96
```

Let's convert it to an Int.

```
let i = Int(d)
```

And print it out...

```
print("Result: \(i)")
```

How It Works

In order to convert a double to Int, we can easily use the Int initializer.

```
Result: 18
```

10-26. Convert double to string

Problem

I want to convert a given double number to its string representation.

Solution

Let's create our test double.

```
let a : Double = 6.2
```

Let's convert it to a string.

```
let str = String(a)
```

And print it out...

```
print("Result: \(str)")
```

How It Works

In order to convert a double to string, we can easily use the `String` initializer.

```
Result: 6.2
```

10-27. Convert float to CGFloat

Problem

I want to convert a Float number to a CGFloat.

Solution

```
import Foundation
```

Let's create our test number.

```
let f : Float = 18.96
```

Let's convert it to a CGFloat.

```
let cf = CGFloat(f)
```

And print it out...

```
print("Result: \(cf)")
```

How It Works

In order to convert a Float to CGFloat, we can easily use the CGFloat initializer.

```
Result: 18.9599990844727
```

10-28. Convert float to integer
Problem

I want to convert a float number to an Int.

Solution

Let's create our test number.

```
let f : Float = 18.96
```

Let's convert it to an Int.

```
let i = Int(f)
```

And print it out...

```
print("Result: \(i)")
```

How It Works

In order to convert a float to int, we can easily use the `Int` initializer.

```
Result: 18
```

10-29. Convert float to string
Problem

I want to convert a float number to its string representation.

Solution

Let's create our test floating-point number.

```
let a : Float = 4.3
```

Let's convert it to a string.

```
let str = String(a)
```

And print it out...

```
print("Result: \(str)")
```

How It Works

In order to convert a float to string, we can easily use the `String` initializer.

```
Result: 4.3
```

10-30. Convert integer to double

Problem

I want to convert an int number to double.

Solution

Let's create our test number.

```
let i = 11
```

Let's convert it to a Double.

```
let d = Double(i)
```

And print it out...

```
print("Result: \(d)")
```

How It Works

In order to convert an int to double, we can easily use the double initializer.

```
Result: 11.0
```

10-31. Convert integer to float

Problem

I want to convert an int number to float.

Solution

Let's create our test number.

```
let i = 16
```

Let's convert it to a float.

```
let f = Float(i)
```

And print it out...

```
print("Result: \(f)")
```

How It Works

In order to convert an int to float, we can easily use the Float initializer.

```
Result: 16.0
```

10-32. Convert integer to string

Problem

I want to convert an int number to its string representation.

Solution

Let's create our test integer.

```
let a : Int = 6
```

Let's convert it to a string.

```
let str = String(a)
```

And print it out...

```
print("Result: \(str)")
```

How It Works

In order to convert an int to string, we can easily use the String initializer.

```
Result: 6
```

10-33. Convert radians to degrees

Problem

I want to convert an angle, from radians to degrees.

Solution

```
import Foundation
```

Let's set our test value.

```
let radians = 0.3
```

Then, we convert it to degrees.

```
let degrees = radians * 180 / Double.pi
```

And print out the result...

```
print("\(radians) radians = \(degrees) degrees")
```

How It Works

In order to convert radians to degrees, we can use the known formula:
```
d = r * 180 / pi
```

```
0.3 radians = 17.188733853924695 degrees
```

10-34. Generate a random number within range

Problem

I want to generate a random number within a specific range.

Solution

```
import Foundation
```

Let's generate our random number. We want a random number between 2 and 10 (not including 10).

```
let rand = Int.random(in: 2..10)
```

And... print it out.

```
print("Our random number is: \(rand)")
```

How It Works

In order to generate a random number, within a specific range, we'll be using the Int.random(in:) function.

```
Our random number is: 7
```

10-35. Generate a random number

Problem

I want to generate any random number.

Solution

```
import Foundation
```

Let's generate our random number.

```
let rand = Int.random(in:0..1000)
```

And... print it out.

```
print("Our random number is: \(rand)")
```

How It Works

In order to generate a random number, we'll be using the `Int.random(in:)` function.

```
Our random number is: 18
```

10-36. Get absolute value of number

Problem

I want to get the absolute value of a given number.

Solution

First, let's take a test number.

```
let x = -10
```

Then, we get its absolute value.

```
let absolute = abs(x)
```

And print it out...

```
print("The absolute value of \(x) is: \(absolute)")
```

How It Works

In order to get the absolute value of a number, we can use the abs function.

```
The absolute value of -10 is: 10
```

10-37. Get maximum of two values
Problem

I want to get the maximum of two given values.

Solution

First, let's take some test numbers.

```
let a = 5
let b = -2
```

Then, we calculate their maximum.

```
let maximum = max(a, b)
```

And print it out...

```
print("The maximum is: \(maximum)")
```

How It Works

In order to get the maximum of two given values, we can use the max function.

```
The maximum is: 5
```

10-38. Get minimum of two values

Problem

I want to get the minimum of two given values.

Solution

First, let's take some test numbers.

```
let a = -10
let b = 6
```

Then, we calculate their minimum.

```
let minimum = min(a, b)
```

And print it out...

```
print("The minimum is: \(minimum)")
```

How It Works

In order to get the maximum of two given values, we can use the `min` function.

```
The minimum is: -10
```

10-39. Round decimal down to whole number

Problem

I want to round a given decimal value down to a whole number.

Solution

```
import Foundation
```

First, we set our test numbers.

```
let a = 1.21
let b = 1.42
let c = 1.73
```

What about rounding them?

```
let roundA = floor(a)
let roundB = floor(b)
let roundC = floor(c)
```

Let's print the results...

```
print("\(a) => \(roundA)")
print("\(b) => \(roundB)")
print("\(c) => \(roundC)")
```

How It Works

In order to round a decimal number down to a whole number, we may use the floor function.

```
1.21 => 1.0
1.42 => 1.0
1.73 => 1.0
```

10-40. Round decimal to nearest whole number

Problem

I want to round a given decimal value to the nearest whole number.

Solution

```
import Foundation
```

First, we set our test numbers.

```
let a = 1.21
let b = 1.42
let c = 1.73
```

What about rounding them?

```
let roundA = round(a)
let roundB = round(b)
let roundC = round(c)
```

Let's print the results...

```
print("\(a) => \(roundA)")
print("\(b) => \(roundB)")
print("\(c) => \(roundC)")
```

How It Works

In order to round a decimal number to the nearest whole number, we may use the round function.

```
1.21 => 1.0
1.42 => 1.0
1.73 => 2.0
```

10-41. Round decimal up to whole number

Problem

I want to round a given decimal value up to a whole number.

Solution

```
import Foundation
```

First, we set our test numbers.

```
let a = 1.21
let b = 1.42
let c = 1.73
```

What about rounding them?

```
let roundA = ceil(a)
let roundB = ceil(b)
let roundC = ceil(c)
```

Let's print the results...

```
print("\(a) => \(roundA)")
print("\(b) => \(roundB)")
print("\(c) => \(roundC)")
```

How It Works

In order to round a decimal number up to a whole number, we may use the ceil function.

```
1.21 => 2.0
1.42 => 2.0
1.73 => 2.0
```

10-42. Calculate date after adding to date

Problem

I want to calculate the resulting date after adding an interval to a given date.

Solution

```
import Foundation
```

First, we keep a reference to our current date – that is: now.

```
let now = Date()
```

Let's say we want to get the date, 10 days from now. That is: We'll add 10 days to our current date.

```
let futureDate = Calendar.current.date(byAdding: .day, value:
10, to: now)
```

Let's print that future date...

```
print("10 days from now: \(futureDate!)")
```

How It Works

In order to calculate a date, based on a given date object, after some time has passed, we can use the current Calendar's, date(byAdding:value:to:) method.

```
10 days from now: 2017-03-21 11:38:47 +0000
```

10-43. Check if date is in the future

Problem

I want to check if a given date is in the future.

Solution

```
import Foundation
```

First, we set our given date to some test date.

```
let formatter = DateFormatter()
formatter.dateFormat = "yyyy-MM-dd"
```

```
let date = formatter.date(from: "1986-10-27")
```

Then we keep a reference to our current date – that is: now.

```
let now = Date()
```

Time to compare them.

Note   date is an optional. But in this case, it's rather safe to force-unwrap it.

```
if date! > now {
     print("Yes, it's in the future.")
} else {
     print("No, it's not in the future.")
}
```

How It Works

In order to check if a specific Date object is in the future, we can simply compare it with our current date.

```
No, it's not in the future.
```

10-44. Check if date is in the past

Problem

I want to check if a given date is in the past.

Solution

```
import Foundation
```

First, we set our given date to some test date.

```
let formatter = DateFormatter()
formatter.dateFormat = "yyyy-MM-dd"

let date = formatter.date(from: "1986-10-27")
```

Then we keep a reference to our current date – that is: now.

```
let now = Date()
```

Time to compare them.

Note   a is an optional. But in this case, it's rather safe to force-unwrap it.

```
if date! < now {
    print("Yes, it's in the past.")
} else {
    print("No, it's not in the past.")
}
```

How It Works

In order to check if a specific Date object is in the past, we can simply compare it with our current date.

```
Yes, it's in the past.
```

10-45. Check if date is today
Problem

I want to check if a given date is today.

Solution

```
import Foundation
```

First, we set our given date to some test date.

```
let formatter = DateFormatter()
formatter.dateFormat = "yyyy-MM-dd"
```

```
let a = formatter.date(from: "1986-10-27")
```

Then we keep a reference to our current date – that is: now.

```
let b = Date()
```

Then, we extract the desired components from each date, namely: year, month, and day.

```
let dateToCheck = Calendar.current.dateComponents([.year,
.month, .day], from: a!)
let currentDate = Calendar.current.dateComponents([.year,
.month, .day], from: b)
```

Time to check if they coincide.

```
if dateToCheck.year   == currentDate.year &&
   dateToCheck.month == currentDate.month &&
   dateToCheck.day    == currentDate.day {
      print("Yep, it's today.")
} else {
      print("Well, this date we gave me... it's not today!")
}
```

How It Works

In order to check if a specific Date object is today, we can use the DateComponents class to retrieve the different components of the given date, and then compare them with our current date.

```
Well, this date we gave me... it's not today!
```

10-46. Check if two dates are equal
Problem

I want to check if two different dates are equal.

Solution

```
import Foundation
```

First, we initialize our dates.

```
let a = Date()
```

Note   This is not the same as above. A few milliseconds have passed, so it's a 100% distinct date ;-)

```
let b = Date()
```

Now, let's see...

```
if a == b {
    print("Yes, they are the same.")
} else {
    print("Nope, they are not equal - wait, what?!")
}
```

How It Works

To compare two dates and check if they are equal, we can use the ==
comparison operator. (The result of this specific example may, at times,
differ in the given the different CPU time spent creating both date objects).

```
Nope, they are not equal - wait, what?!
```

10-47. Compare two dates

Problem

I want to compare two different dates.

Solution

```
import Foundation
```

First, we initialize our dates.

```
let a = Date()
```

Note   This is not the same as above.

A few milliseconds have passed, so it's a 100% distinct date ;-)

```
let b = Date()
```

Now, let's see...

```
if a < b {
        print("Date A comes before Date B")
}else {
        print("Date B comes before Date A")
}
```

How It Works

To compare two dates - that is: which one *would* come first, we can use the < and > comparison operators.

```
Date A comes before Date B
```

10-48. Create date from current date

Problem

I want to create a date object from the current date.

Solution

```
import Foundation
```

Let's create our date.

```
let now = Date()
```

And print it out – yes, it was that simple!

```
print("Current date: \(now)")
```

How It Works

In order to create a new date object for the current date and time we can use date's initializer.

```
Current date: 2017-03-11 11:38:49 +0000
```

10-49. Create date from given date

Problem

I want to create a date object from a given date.

Solution

```
import Foundation
```

First, we set our desired year/month/day.

```
var date = DateComponents()
date.year = 2016
date.month = 10
date.day = 27
```

Then, we create our NSDate object.

```
let dateObj = Calendar.current.date(from: date)
```

And print it out.

Note   It's optional, but there is no harm force-unwrapping it in this particular case.

```
print("Given date: \(dateObj!)")
```

How It Works

In order to create a new Date object, for a given year/month/day, we can use the DateComponents class, along with the current Calendar.

```
Given date: 2016-10-26 22:00:00 +0000
```

10-50. Create date from given string format
Problem

I want to create a Date object from a given string format.

Solution

```
import Foundation
```

First, we set a test date string.

```
let dateString = "2016-10-27"
```

Then, we initialize a DateFormatter and set a date format.

```
let formatter = DateFormatter()
formatter.dateFormat = "yyyy-MM-dd"
```

Lastly, we convert our date to a date object.

```
let date = formatter.date(from: dateString)
```

Let's see what we've managed...

Note   It's optional, but there is no harm in force-unwrapping it in this particular case.

```
print("Date: \(date!)")
```

How It Works

In order to create a new date object, from a given formatted string, we can use the DateFormatter class.

```
Date: 2016-10-26 22:00:00 +0000
```

10-51. Find date in string

Problem

I want to find a date in a specific string.

Solution

```
import Foundation
```

Let's set some example text.

```
let text = "This is a random date: 03/01/2017"
```

Let's create our detector. We want the dates, so we'll look for this: NSTextCheckingResult.CheckingType.date.rawValue.

```
let detector = try! NSDataDetector(types: NSTextCheckingResult.
CheckingType.date.rawValue)
let results = detector.matches(in: text, options: [], range:
NSRange(location: 0, length: text.count))
```

Loop through the dates we found.

```
for result in results {

    // And print them out

    print(result.date!)

}
```

How It Works

In order to find a date within some text, we may use the NSDataSelector class.

```
2017-03-01 11:00:00 +0000
```

10-52. Format string from date

Problem

I want to format a string from a given date.

Solution

```
import Foundation
```

First, we set our date – to... now.

```
let date = Date()
```

Then, we initialize a DateFormatter and set a date format.

```
let formatter = DateFormatter()
formatter.dateFormat = "yyyy-MM-dd"
```

Lastly, we convert our date to a date string.

```
let dateStr = formatter.string(from: date)
```

Let's see what we've managed...

```
print("Date: \(dateStr)")
```

How It Works

In order to get a string for a given date, we can use the DateFormatter class.

```
Date: 2017-03-11
```

10-53. Get components from date

Problem

I want to get the different components of a given date.

Solution

```
import Foundation
```

First, we set our desired date – to... now.

```
var date = Date()
```

Then, we extract the desired components, namely: year, month, and day.

```
let components = Calendar.current.dateComponents([.year,
.month, .day], from: date)
```

Let's see what we've got...

Note   All of the data is optional, but in this particular case, it's rather safe to force-unwrap them.

```
print("Year: \(components.year!)")
print("Month: \(components.month!)")
print("Day: \(components.day!)")
```

How It Works

In order to get a Date's individual components, for example, day, month, year, we can use the `DateComponents` class.

```
Year: 2018
Month: 10
Day: 8
```

10-54. Get day from date

Problem

I want to get the day component of a given date.

Solution

```
import Foundation
```

First, we set our desired date – to... now.

```
var date = Date()
```

Then, we extract the desired component, that is: the day.

```
let day = Calendar.current.component(.day, from: date)
```

Let's print it out...

```
print("Current day: \(day)")
```

How It Works

In order to get the day from a Date object, we can use the current Calendar's `component(_:from:)` method.

```
Current day: 11
```

10-55. Get days difference between dates

Problem

I want to get the difference, in days, between two different dates.

Solution

```
import Foundation
```

First, we create our Date objects.

```
let formatter = DateFormatter()
formatter.dateFormat = "yyyy-MM-dd"

let a = formatter.date(from: "1986-10-27")
let b = formatter.date(from: "2016-12-30")
```

We want the difference in days. So we set that to: `.day`

Note   Other possible values: `.year, .month, .day, .hour, .minute, .nanosecond`

```
let unit : Calendar.Component = .day
```

Time to get their difference.

```
let start = Calendar.current.ordinality(of: unit, in: .era,
for: a!)
let end = Calendar.current.ordinality(of: unit, in: .era, for: b!)
```

They are both optional, but in this case it's pretty safe to force-unwrap them.

```
let diff = end! - start!
```

And let's print the result...

```
print("Difference: \(diff) days")
```

How It Works

In order to calculate the difference in seconds between two different Date objects, we may use the current Calendar and its ordinality(of:in:for:) method.

```
Difference: 11022 days
```

10-56. Get month from date
Problem

I want to get the month component of a given date.

Solution

```
import Foundation
```

First, we set our desired date – to... now.

```
var date = Date()
```

Then, we extract the desired component, that is: the month.

```
let month = Calendar.current.component(.month, from: date)
```

Let's print it out...

```
print("Current month: \(month)")
```

How It Works

In order to get the month from a date object, we can use the current Calendar's component(_:from:) method.

```
Current month: 3
```

10-57. Get month name from date
Problem

I want to get the month name component of a given date.

Solution

```
import Foundation
```

First, we set our desired date – to... now.

```
var date = Date()
```

Then, we extract the desired component, that is: the month.

```
let month = Calendar.current.component(.month, from: date)
```

And match it to the appropriate name.

```
let months = ["January", "February", "March", "April", "May",
"June",
                      "July", "August", "September", "October",
"November", "December"]

let monthName = months[month-1]
```

Let's print it out...

```
print("Current month: \(monthName)")
```

How It Works

In order to get the month name from a Date object, we can use the current Calendar's component(_:from:) method.

```
Current month: March
```

10-58. Get seconds difference between times

Problem

I want to get the difference, in seconds, between two different times.

Solution

```
import Foundation
```

First, we create our date objects with a delay of 2 seconds in between.

```
let a = Date()
sleep(2)
let b = Date()
```

We want the difference in seconds. So we set that to: `.second`.

Note   Other possible values: `.year`, `.month`, `.day`, `.hour`, `.minute`, `.nanosecond`

```
let unit : Calendar.Component = .second
```

Time to get their difference

```
let start = Calendar.current.ordinality(of: unit, in: .year,
for: a)
let end = Calendar.current.ordinality(of: unit, in: .year, for: b)
```

They are both optional, but in this case it's pretty safe to force-unwrap them.

```
let diff = end! - start!
```

And let's print the result...

```
print("Difference: \(diff) seconds")
```

How It Works

In order to calculate the difference in seconds between two different Date objects, we may use the current Calendar and its `ordinality(of:in:for:)` method.

```
Difference: 2 seconds
```

10-59. Get Unix timestamp for current date
Problem

I want to get the Unix timestamp for the current date.

Solution

```
import Foundation
```

Let's create our date.

```
let now = Date()
```

Get the timestamp.

```
let timestamp = now.timeIntervalSince1970
```

And print it out – yes, it was that simple.

```
print("Current Unix timestamp: \(timestamp)")
```

How It Works

In order to get the Unix timestamp for the current date, we have to create a new Date object, for current date and time, and its timeIntervalSince1970 property.

```
Current Unix timestamp: 1489232335.80579
```

10-60. Get year from date
Problem

I want to get the year component of a given date.

Solution

```
import Foundation
```

First, we set our desired date – to... now.

```
var date = Date()
```

Then, we extract the desired component, that is: the year.

```
let year = Calendar.current.component(.year, from: date)
```

Let's print it out...

```
print("Current year: \(year)")
```

How It Works

In order to get the year from a Date object, we can use the current Calendar's `component(_:from:)` method.

```
Current year: 2018
```

10-61. Summary

In this chapter, we learned how we can make the most out of numbers and dates.

In the next one, we'll be looking into Errors and Exceptions: that is, how we can create our own custom types and be able to predict and prevent different – unpleasant – scenarios during our app's execution.

CHAPTER 11

Exceptions

Execution-time errors – or, in programming, Exceptions – are a rather normal, even though unpleasant, thing of every coder's life. However, they can be prevented – or at least, at times. This is where Error Handling comes into play.

Error handling is nothing but a fancy name to describe the process of responding to the occurrence, during computation, of exceptions – anomalous conditions, that is, that may require some special processing. And Swift sure makes our life a lot easier.

11-1. Create a custom error
Problem

I want to create a new custom error type.

Solution

Let's create our custom error type.

```
enum myError : Error {
    case seriousError
    case notSoSeriousError
}
```

...and let's throw some error to see that it works.

```
throw myError.seriousError
```

What's going to happen? The program will crash.

And that means: it worked! Yay!

How It Works

An Error type is nothing but an enumeration of possible error values, conforming to the Error protocol. By using the throw command, we can invoke a particular exception.

11-2. Throw and catch a custom error

Problem

I want to throw and catch a new custom error type.

Solution

Let's create our custom error type.

```
enum myError : Error {
    case seriousError
    case notSoSeriousError
}
```

We include the not-so-safe code in a do-catch block if something goes wrong, then we're ready to "catch" the possible exceptions.

```
do {
    // Not the way you'd normally do, since it'll throw an
    error anyway,
    // but good and simple enough to see that it works

    throw myError.seriousError
}
catch myError.seriousError {
    print("Oops: Just caught a serious error!")
}
catch myError.notSoSeriousError {
    print("Oops: Just caught a not-so-serious error")
}
```

What's going to happen? The app will quit – but do so... gracefully.

How It Works

An error type is nothing but an enumeration of possible error values, conforming to the Error protocol. By using the throw command, we can invoke a particular exception. And by using the catch command, we can *catch* the different exceptions and handle the various scenarios - safely.

```
Oops: Just caught a serious error!
```

11-3. Create a custom error with associated values
Problem

I want to create a new custom error type with different associated values.

Solution

Let's create our custom error type. Our second error will also include an associated value.

```
enum myError : Error {
    case seriousError
    case anotherError(String)
}
```

...and let's throw some error, with a value/message, to see that it works.

```
throw myError.anotherError("something went really really wrong!")
```

What's going to happen? The program will crash.
And that means: it worked! Yay!

How It Works

We already know about errors. But what if, instead of just having an error, we can also associate a "value" with it, mainly for informative purposes? Sound useful, doesn't it?

11-4. Call throwing function and catch custom error

Problem

I want to call a throwing function and catch some custom error type.

Solution

Let's create our custom error type.

```
enum operationError : Error {
    case numberTooLarge
    case divisionByZero
}
```

Here's our simple function, which takes two arguments and returns the result of their integer division.

```
func performDivision(_ a : Int, _ b : Int) throws -> Int {
    if b == 0 {
        throw operationError.divisionByZero
    }
    else if a > 100000 {
        throw operationError.numberTooLarge
    }
    else {
        return a / b
    }
}
```

We include the not-so-safe code in a do-catch block, if something goes wrong, then we're ready to "catch" the possible exceptions.

```
do {
    // Since it's a function that "throws",
    // we have to put a "try" in front of it

    let result = try performDivision(5, 0)

    print("The result is: \(result)")
}
```

```
catch operationError.numberTooLarge {
    print("Oops: Number > 100000. That was too large for me!")
}
catch operationError.divisionByZero {
    print("Oops: Tried to divide by zero. Are you out of your
    mind?")
}
```

How It Works

An Error type is nothing but an enumeration of possible error values, conforming to the Error protocol. This time we'll write a function that possibly throws a custom error and, on the side, be ready to catch it.

```
Oops: Tried to divide by zero. Are you out of your mind?
```

11-5. Call throwing function and convert errors to optionals

Problem

I want to call a throwing function and convert the different errors to optional values.

Solution

Another way, though, is by converting the error to an "optional" value: that is, if everything goes as planned, we get the value of the function; otherwise, we get nil.

Let's create a custom error type.

```
enum operationError : Error {
    case numberTooLarge
    case divisionByZero
}
```

Here's our simple function, which may throw an error.

```
func performDivision(_ a : Int, _ b : Int) throws -> Int {

    guard b != 0 else { throw operationError.divisionByZero }
    guard a < 100000 else { throw operationError.
    numberTooLarge }

    return a/b
}
```

Let's call our function.

To make sure nothing goes wrong, instead of enclosing it in a do-catch block, we'll just put a 'try?' in front of the throwing function call to convert it to an optional.

That's all.

```
let result = try? performDivision(5, 2)
```

Time to print the result...

```
print("Result: \(String(describing:result))")
```

How It Works

A throwing function is one that can possibly throw an error. The "normal" way of handling this is by enclosing the call to that function in a *do-catch* block, and try to catch all possible errors.

```
Result: Optional(2)
```

11-6. Create throwing function with guard statements and catch custom error

Problem

I want to create a throwing function with various guard statements and catch a custom error type.

Solution

Let's create our custom error type.

```
enum operationError : Error {
    case numberTooLarge
    case divisionByZero
}
```

Here's our simple function, which takes two arguments and returns the result of their integer division.

```
func performDivision(_ a : Int, _ b : Int) throws -> Int {

    // We'll use 'guard' statements to first verify
    everything goes as planned
    // If there's anything wrong, we'll throw the appropriate
    error.

    guard b != 0 else { throw operationError.divisionByZero }
    guard a < 100000 else { throw operationError.
    numberTooLarge }

    // Otherwise, we'll proceed with the division

    return a/b
}
```

We include the not-so-safe code in a do-catch block if something goes wrong, then we're ready to "catch" the possible exceptions.

```
do {

    // Since it's a function that "throws",
    // we have to put a "try" in front of it

    let result = try performDivision(5, 0)

    print("The result is: \(result)")
}
catch operationError.numberTooLarge {
    print("Oops: Number > 100000. That was too large for me!")
}
catch operationError.divisionByZero {
    print("Oops: Tried to divide by zero. Are you out of your
    mind?")
}
```

How It Works

This time we'll write a function that possibly throws a custom error, using guard statements, and, on the side, be ready to catch it! :).

```
Oops: Tried to divide by zero. Are you out of your mind?
```

11-7. Write assertions based on condition
Problem

I want to write different assertions based on some given conditions.

Solution

Let's set some test variables.

```
let number = 6
let divisor = 3
```

Let's make 100% sure the divisor is not a zero.

```
assert(divisor != 0, "Divisor zero. I'm sorry but I cannot
continue")
```

Here we are. So, let's perform the division.

```
print("The result of the division is \(number/divisor)")
```

How It Works

Assertions are an easy way to verify a specific (necessary) condition has been met. Or, if not, the application will terminate. For that reason, we may use the `assert` function.

```
The result of the division is 2
```

11-8. Summary

In this chapter, we learned how we can create our own error types; and throw and catch errors, which can make our applications even safer.

In the next one, we'll go one step deeper and start exploring the file system; reading and writing files, or getting useful system information; as well as learn how we can interact with the Web, by making HTTP requests.

CHAPTER 12

Web, Files, and System

There is virtually no solid application that doesn't need some level of file access and/or web access nowadays.

In this chapter, we'll be looking at what Swift offers us and how we can easily play with files, read/write to them, retrieve useful information from our user's system, and even take it one step further and interact with the WWW.

12-1. Check if file exists

Problem

I want to check if a specific file exists.

Solution

```
import Foundation
```

Let's set our file path.

```
let path = "tests/hello.swift"
```

And check if it exists.

```
if FileManager.default.fileExists(atPath: path) {
    print("Yes, the file does exist!")
} else {
    print("Nope, the file does not exist.")
}
```

How It Works

In order to check if a particular file exists at a given path, we may use FileManager's fileExists(atPath:) method.

```
Nope, the file does not exist.
```

12-2. Check if file is deletable
Problem

I want to check if a specific file can be deleted.

Solution

```
import Foundation
```

Let's set our file path.

```
let path = "tests/hello.swift"
```

And check if it is deletable.

```
if FileManager.default.isDeletableFile(atPath: path) {
    print("Yes, the file is deletable!")
} else {
    print("Nope, the file is not deletable.")
}
```

How It Works

In order to check if a particular file at a given path is deletable, we may use FileManager's isDeletableFile(atPath:) method.

```
Yes, the file is deletable!
```

12-3. Check if file is executable

Problem

I want to check if a specific file can be executed.

Solution

```
import Foundation
```

Let's set our file path.

```
let path = "tests/hello.swift"
```

And check if it is executable.

```
if FileManager.default.isExecutableFile(atPath: path) {
    print("Yes, the file is executable!")
} else {
    print("Nope, the file is not executable.")
}
```

How It Works

In order to check if a particular file at a given path is executable, we may use FileManager's isExecutableFile(atPath:) method.

```
Nope, the file is not executable.
```

12-4. Check if file is readable

Problem

I want to check if a specific file can be read.

Solution

```
import Foundation
```

Let's set our file path.

Note   For this code to work, we must obviously have some file already created at tests/hello.swift.

```
let path = "tests/hello.swift"
```

And check if it is readable.

```
if FileManager.default.isReadableFile(atPath: path) {
    print("Yes, the file is readable!")
} else {
    print("Nope, the file is not readable.")
}
```

How It Works

In order to check if a particular file at a given path is readable, we may use FileManager's isReadableFile(atPath:) method.

```
Yes, the file is readable!
```

12-5. Check if file is writable

Problem

I want to check if a specific file can be written to.

Solution

```
import Foundation
```

Let's set our file path.

```
let path = "tests/hello.swift"
```

And check if it is writable.

```
if FileManager.default.isWritableFile(atPath: path) {
    print("Yes, the file is writable!")
} else {
    print("Nope, the file is not writable.")
}
```

How It Works

In order to check if a particular file at a given path is writable, we may use FileManager's isWritableFile(atPath:) method.

```
Nope, the file is not writable.
```

12-6. Check if path is folder

Problem

I want to check if a given path corresponds to a folder.

Solution

```
import Foundation
```

Let's set our file path.

```
let path = "tests"
```

We'll need an ObjCBool variable to store the Boolean, that is: whether the directory exists or not.

```
var isFolder : ObjCBool = false

let _ = FileManager.default.fileExists(atPath: path,
isDirectory: &isFolder)
```

Let's see if it's a folder then.

```
if isFolder.boolValue {
    print("Yes, the path points to a folder!")
} else {
    print("Well, either that path points to a file, or the
    file doesn't exist whatsoever")
}
```

How It Works

In order to check if a particular path refers to a folder (and not a file), we may use FileManager's fileExists(atPath:isDirectory:) method.

```
Yes, the path points to a folder!
```

12-7. Copy file to path

Problem

I want to copy a file at a given path to another path.

Solution

```
import Foundation
```

Let's set our paths:
- The file path we're copying from
- And the new file path we're copying it to

```
let pathFrom = "tests/fileToCopy.txt"
let pathTo   = "tests/new/location/fileToCopy.txt"
```

Time to create our folder.

```
do {
    try FileManager.default.copyItem(atPath: pathFrom,
    toPath: pathTo)

    print("Yep, file was successfully copied!")
}
catch let error {
    print("Ooops! Something went wrong: \(error)")
}
```

How It Works

If we want to copy a particular file at a given path to another location, we may use FileManager's copyItem(atPath:toPath) method.

```
Yep, file was successfully copied!
```

12-8. Create directory at path

Problem

I want to create a specific directory at a given path.

Solution

```
import Foundation
```

Let's set our (new) folder path.

```
let path = "tests/folder/to/create"
```

Time to create our folder.

```
do {
    try FileManager.default.createDirectory(atPath: path,
    withIntermediateDirectories: true, attributes: [:])

    print("Yep, directory was successfully created!")
}
catch let error {
    print("Ooops! Something went wrong: \(error)")
}
```

How It Works

If we want to create a particular folder at a given path, we may use
FileManager's createDirectory method.

```
Yep, directory was successfully created!
```

12-9. Create URL from file path

Problem

I want to create a URL object from a given file path.

Solution

```
import Foundation
```

First, we initialize our example file path.

```
let path = "/var/www/html/indcx.html"
```

Then, we convert it to a URL.

```
let url = URL(fileURLWithPath: path)
```

And... let's print it out.

```
print("URL: \(url)")
```

How It Works

In order to convert/bridge a file path string to a URL, we can use the `URL(fileURLWithPath:)` initializer.

```
URL: file:///var/www/html/index.html
```

12-10. Create URL from string

Problem

I want to create a URL object from a given string.

Solution

```
import Foundation
```

First, we initialize our example URL string.

```
let urlString = "https://iswift.org"
```

Then, we convert it to a URL.

```
let url = URL(string: urlString)
```

And... let's print it out.

```
print("URL: \(String(describing:url))")
```

How It Works

In order to convert/bridge a file path string to a URL, we can use the URL(string:) initializer.

```
URL: Optional(https://iswift.org)
```

12-11. Delete file at path

Problem

I want to delete a file at a specific file path.

Solution

```
import Foundation
```

Let's set our file path.

```
let path = "tests/fileToDelete.txt"
```

Time to delete our file.

```
do {
    try FileManager.default.removeItem(atPath: path)

    print("Yep, file was successfully deleted!")
}
catch let error {
    print("Ooops! Something went wrong: \(error)")
}
```

How It Works

If we want to delete a particular file at a given path, we may use
FileManager's removeItem(atPath:) method.

```
Yep, file was successfully deleted!
```

12-12. Delete folder at path
Problem

I want to delete a folder at a specific file path.

Solution

```
import Foundation
```

Let's set our folder path.

```
let path = "tests/folderToDelete"
```

Time to delete our folder.

```
do {
    try FileManager.default.removeItem(atPath: path)

    print("Yep, folder was successfully deleted!")
}
catch let error {
    print("Ooops! Something went wrong: \(error)")
}
```

How It Works

If we want to delete a particular folder at a given path, we may use FileManager's removeItem(atPath:) method, as you'd normally do for a simple file.

```
Yep, folder was successfully deleted!
```

12-13. Extract file extension from path string

Problem

I want to get the file extension component of a given path string.

Solution

```
import Foundation
```

First, we set our test path.

```
let path = URL(fileURLWithPath: "/var/www/index.html")
```

Then, we extract the extension.

```
let ext = path.pathExtension
```

And print it out...

```
print("Result: \(ext)")
```

How It Works

In order to extract the file extension from a given path string, we'll have to convert our string to a URL using URL(fileURLWithPath:), and then use the pathExtension property.

```
Result: html
```

12-14. Extract filename from path string

Problem

I want to get the filename component of a given path string.

Solution

```
import Foundation
```

First, we set our test path.

```
let path = URL(fileURLWithPath: "/var/www/index.html")
```

Then, we extract the filename.

```
let filename = path.lastPathComponent
```

And print it out...

```
print("Result: \(filename)")
```

How It Works

In order to extract the filename from a given path string, we'll have to convert our string to a URL using URL(fileURLWithPath:), and then use the lastPathComponent property.

Result: index.html

12-15. Extract folder from path string

Problem

I want to get the folder component of a given path string.

Solution

```
import Foundation
```

First, we set our test path.

```
let path = URL(fileURLWithPath: "/var/www/index.html")
```

Then, we extract the filename.

```
let folder = path.deletingLastPathComponent().path
```

And print it out...

```
print("Result: \(folder)")
```

How It Works

In order to extract the folder from a given path string, we'll have to convert our string to a URL using URL(fileURLWithPath:), and then use the deletingLastPathComponent method.

Result: /var/www

12-16. Extract path components from path string

Problem

I want to get the different path components of a given path string.

Solution

```
import Foundation
```

First, we set our test path.

```
let path = URL(fileURLWithPath: "/var/www/index.html")
```

Then, we extract the components.

```
let components = path.pathComponents
```

And print it out...

```
print("Result: \(components)")
```

How It Works

In order to parse the path components of a given path string, we'll have to convert our string to a URL using URL(fileURLWithPath:), and then use the pathComponents property.

```
Result: ["/", "var", "www", "index.html"]
```

12-17. Get attributes of file

Problem

I want to get the different attributes of a given file.

Solution

```
import Foundation
```

Let's set our test file path.

```
let path = "tests/hello.swift"
```

Time to get our file size.

```
do {
    // First we get the file attributes

    let attrs = try FileManager.default.
    attributesOfItem(atPath: path)

    // And print out the result

    print("Attributes: \(attrs)")

}
catch let error {
    print("Ooops! Something went wrong: \(error)")
}
```

How It Works

If we want to get the attributes of a specific file at a given path, we may use FileManager's attributesOfItem(atPath:) method.

```
Attributes: [__C.FileAttributeKey(_rawValue:
NSFileOwnerAccountName): drkameleon, __C.FileAttributeKey
(_rawValue: NSFilePosixPermissions): 420, __C.
FileAttributeKey(_rawValue: NSFileSystemNumber): 16777217,
__C.FileAttributeKey(_rawValue: NSFileReferenceCount): 1,
__C.FileAttributeKey(_rawValue: NSFileSystemFileNumber):
45429771, __C.FileAttributeKey(_rawValue: NSFileCreationDate):
2017-03-18 07:29:35 +0000, __C.FileAttributeKey(_rawValue:
NSFileHFSTypeCode): 0, __C.FileAttributeKey(_rawValue:
NSFileType): NSFileTypeRegular, __C.FileAttributeKey(_rawValue:
NSFileExtendedAttributes): {
    "com.apple.metadata:_kMDItemUserTags" = <62706c69 73743030
a0080000 00000000 01010000 00000000 00010000 00000000 00000000
00000000 0009>;
}, __C.FileAttributeKey(_rawValue:
NSFileGroupOwnerAccountName): admin, __C.FileAttributeKey
(_rawValue: NSFileGroupOwnerAccountID): 80, __C.
FileAttributeKey(_rawValue: NSFileHFSCreatorCode): 0, __C.
FileAttributeKey(_rawValue: NSFileModificationDate): 2017-03-
18 07:29:45 +0000, __C.FileAttributeKey(_rawValue: NSFileSize):
23, __C.FileAttributeKey(_rawValue: NSFileExtensionHidden): 0,
__C.FileAttributeKey(_rawValue: NSFileOwnerAccountID): 501]
```

12-18. Get current directory path
Problem

I want to get the current directory path.

Solution

```
import Foundation
```

Let's get our current path.

```
let currentPath = FileManager.default.currentDirectoryPath
```

And print it out...

```
print("Current path: \(currentPath)")
```

How It Works

If we want to get our current directory path, we may use FileManager's currentDirectoryPath property.

```
Current path: /tmp/test/swift
```

12-19. Get directory contents at path

Problem

I want to get the contents of a directory at given path as an array.

Solution

```
import Foundation
```

Let's set our file path.

```
let path = "tests"
```

Time to get our paths.

```
do {
    let contents = try FileManager.default.
    subpathsOfDirectory(atPath: path)

    // And print them out

    print(contents)
}
catch let error {
    print("Ooops! Something went wrong: \(error)")
}
```

How It Works

If we want to get all of a specific path's content paths, files/directories/
everything, we may use FileManager's subpathsOfDirectory(atPath:)
method.

```
["folder", "folder/to", "folder/to/subfolder", "output.data",
"output.swift"]
```

12-20. Get resource path from bundle
Problem

I want to get the resource's path of a given bundle.

Solution

```
import Foundation
```

Let's get our resource path.

```
if let path = Bundle.main.path(forResource: "myResource",
ofType: "json") {

    // Print it out

    print("Path: \(path)")
} else {

    print("Error getting path for given resource.")
}
```

How It Works

In order to get full path for a given resource file in our app bundle, we may use Bundle's path(forResource:ofType:) method.

```
Error getting path for given resource.
```

12-21. Get size of file

Problem

I want to get the size of a specific file.

Solution

```
import Foundation
```

Let's set our test file path.

```
let path = "tests/hello.swift"
```

Time to get our filesize.

```
do {
    // First we get the file attributes

    let attrs = try FileManager.default.
    attributesOfItem(atPath: path)
    let filesize = (attrs[FileAttributeKey.size] as!
    NSNumber).uint64Value

    // And print out the result

    print("File size: \(filesize)")
}
catch let error {
    print("Ooops! Something went wrong: \(error)")
}
```

How It Works

If we want to get the file size of a specific file at a given path, we may use FileManager's attributesOfItem(atPath:) method.

```
File size: 1520
```

12-22. Move file to path
Problem

I want to move a specific file to a new path.

Solution

```
import Foundation
```

Let's set our paths:

- The file path we're moving

- And the new file path we're moving it to

```
let pathFrom = "tests/fileToMove.txt"
let pathTo   = "tests/new/location/fileToMove.txt"
```

Time to create our folder.

```
do {
    try FileManager.default.moveItem(atPath: pathFrom,
    toPath: pathTo)

    print("Yep, file was successfully moved!")
}
catch let error {
    print("Ooops! Something went wrong: \(error)")
}
```

How It Works

If we want to move a particular file from a given path to another location, we may use FileManager's moveItem(atPath:toPath) method.

```
Yep, file was successfully moved!
```

12-23. Read contents of file into string

Problem

I want to read the contents of a specific text file into a string.

Solution

```
import Foundation
```

First, we set our file path.

```
let path = "tests/hello.swift"
```

Try reading it.

```
do {
    let contents = try String(contentsOfFile: path, encoding:
    .ascii)

    // Yep, we got it! Let's print it out

    print(contents)
}
catch let error {
    print("Ooops! Something went wrong: \(error)")
}
```

How It Works

In order to read a file's content as a string, we may use String's `String(con tentsOfFile:encoding:)` initializer.

```
print("Hello Swift!")
```

12-24. Read data from file

Problem

I want to read the data of a specific file.

Solution

```
import Foundation
```

First, we set our file path.

```
let path = URL(fileURLWithPath: "tests/test.plist")
```

Then, we attempt to read our data.

```
if let data = try? Data(contentsOf: path) {

    // And print it out (not expect much, huh?)

    print("Data: \(data)")

}
```

How It Works

In order to read a file content's as data, we may use the Data(contentsOf:) initializer.

```
<?xml version="1.0" encoding="UTF-8"?>
<!DOCTYPE plist SYSTEM "file://localhost/System/Library/DTDs/
PropertyList.dtd">
<plist version="1.0">
<dict>
    <key>Author</key>
    <string>William Shakespeare</string>
    <key>Lines</key>
    <array>
        <string>It is a tale told by an idiot,</string>
        <string>Full of sound and fury, signifying nothing.</
        string>
```

```
    </array>
    <key>Birthdate</key>
    <integer>1564</integer>
</dict>
</plist>
```

12-25. Rename file at path

Problem

I want to rename a specific file at a given path.

Solution

```
import Foundation
```

Let's set our paths:
- The file path of our file, with its current name
- The new file path, with the new name

```
let pathFrom = "tests/fileToRename.txt"
let pathTo   = "tests/renamedFile.txt"
```

Time to create our folder.

```
do {
    try FileManager.default.moveItem(atPath: pathFrom,
    toPath: pathTo)

    print("Yep, file was successfully renamed!")
}
catch let error {
    print("Ooops! Something went wrong: \(error)")
}
```

How It Works

If we want to rename a particular file at a given path, we may use FileManager's moveItem(atPath:toPath) method, pretty much as we'd do if we wanted it to move it from one location to another.

```
Yep, file was successfully renamed!
```

12-26. Write data to file
Problem

I want to write some data to a specific file.

Solution

```
import Foundation
```

First, we set our file path.

```
let path = URL(fileURLWithPath: "tests/output.data")
```

Then we set our data – from a given string, as an example.

```
let str = "This is some string data\n"

if let data = str.data(using: .utf8) {

    // Let's try writing our file

    do {

        try data.write(to: path)

        print("Yep, we did it! File successfully written.")

    }
```

```
catch let error {
    print("Ooops! Something went wrong: \(error)")
}
}
```

How It Works

In order to write a data object to a file, we may use Data's write(to:) method.

```
Yep, we did it! File successfully written.
```

12-27. Write string contents to file
Problem

I want to write a string to a specific file.

Solution

```
import Foundation
```

First, we set our file path.

```
let path = URL(fileURLWithPath: "tests/output.swift")
```

Then, we set our string.

```
let str = "This is an example string\n"
```

Let's try writing our file...

```
do {
    try str.write(to: path, atomically: true, encoding:
    .ascii)

    print("Yep, we did it! File successfully written.")
}
catch let error {
    print("Ooops! Something went wrong: \(error)")
}
```

How It Works

In order to write a string's contents to a (text) file, we may use String's write(to:atomically:encoding) method.

```
Yep, we did it! File successfully written.
```

12-28. Download web page's HTML into string

Problem

I want to download a specific web page's HTML into a string.

Solution

```
import Foundation
```

First, we set our URL.

```
let url = URL(string: "http://insili.co.uk/iswift/")
```

Try reading it...

```
do {
    let contents = try String(contentsOf: url!, encoding:
    .utf8)

    // Yep, we got it! Let's print it out

    print(contents)
}
catch let error {
    print("Ooops! Something went wrong: \(error)")
}
```

How It Works

In order to download a web page/URL's html content as a string, we may use String's `String(contentsOf:encoding:)` initializer.

```
<h1>Silence is golden.</h1>
```

12-29. Make an HTTP request
Problem

I want to make an HTTP web request.

Solution

```
import Foundation
```

First, we create our URL request.

```
let url = URL(string: "http://insili.co.uk/iswift/get.php")
var req = URLRequest(url: url!)
```

Then we either create a new "session" or use URLSession.shared.

Note   URLSession.shared is not yet implemented for Linux.

```
let session = URLSession(configuration:
URLSessionConfiguration.default)
```

Then, we create the HTTP task.

```
let task = session.dataTask(with: req) { data, response, error
in

    if error != nil {
        print("Error: \(error)")
    } else {
        // Everything went fine
        // Let's check out what the response was

        if let response = response {
            print("Response: \(String(describing:
            response))")
        }

        // And we can also check if there's data for us

        if let data = data,
           let dataStr = String(data: data, encoding:
           .utf8) {
```

```
        // And print the data string too

        print ("Data: \(dataStr)")

    }

  }
}
```

Here, we actually execute the task.

Note   If you forget this step, the task – you created it just fine, yep – but it will never run.

```
task.resume()
```

We have to add some delay here. Otherwise, the app will quit before the server sends a response.

```
sleep(5)
```

How It Works

In order to make an *HTTP GET request*, we may use the URLRequest and URLSession classes, which will help us create an asynchronous task along with its callback.

```
Response: <NSHTTPURLResponse: 0x7f9574c8fcd0> { URL: http://
insili.co.uk/iswift/get.php } { status code: 200, headers {
    Connection = "keep-alive";
    "Content-Encoding" = gzip;
    "Content-Type" = "text/html";
```

```
    Date = "Sat, 11 Mar 2017 11:39:28 GMT";
    Server = "nginx/1.10.3";
    "Transfer-Encoding" = Identity;
} }
Data: <h1>GET request received.</h1>
```

12-30. Make an HTTP request with custom headers

Problem

I want to make an HTTP web request with custom headers.

Solution

```
import Foundation
```

First, we create our URL request.

```
let url = URL(string: "http://insili.co.uk/iswift/get.php")
var req = URLRequest(url: url!)
```

Set our custom request headers.

```
req.addValue("application/json", forHTTPHeaderField:
"Content-Type")
req.addValue("application/json", forHTTPHeaderField: "Accept")
```

Then, we either create a new "session" or use URLSession.shared.

Note   URLSession.shared is not yet implemented for Linux.

```
let session = URLSession(configuration:
URLSessionConfiguration.default)
```

Then, we create the HTTP task.

```
let task = session.dataTask(with: req) { data, response, error
in

    if error != nil {
        print("Error: \(error)")
    } else {

        // Everything went fine
        // Let's check out what the response was

        if let response = response {
            print("Response: \(response)")
        }

        // And we can also check if there's data for us

        if let data = data,
            let dataStr = String(data: data, encoding:
.utf8) {

            // And print the data string too

            print ("Data: \(dataStr)")

        }

    }
}
```

Here, we actually execute the task.

Note   If you forget this step, the task – you created it just fine, yep – but it will never run.

```
task.resume()
```

We have to add some delay here. Otherwise, the app will quit before the server sends a response.

```
sleep(5)
```

How It Works

In order to make an HTTP GET request, we may use the URLRequest and URLSession classes, which will help us create an asynchronous task along with its callback.

```
Response: <NSHTTPURLResponse: 0x7ffa85d5f9c0> { URL: http://
insili.co.uk/iswift/get.php } { status code: 200, headers {
    Connection = "keep-alive";
    "Content-Encoding" = gzip;
    "Content-Type" = "text/html";
    Date = "Sat, 11 Mar 2017 11:39:17 GMT";
    Server = "nginx/1.10.3";
    "Transfer-Encoding" = Identity;
} }
Data: <h1>GET request received.</h1>
```

12-31. Make an HTTP request with JSON data

Problem

I want to make an HTTP web request with JSON data.

Solution

```
import Foundation
```

First, we create our URL request.

```
let url = URL(string: "http://insili.co.uk/iswift/post_json.php")
var req = URLRequest(url: url!)
```

Let's initialize some test JSON data.

```
let json = ["name":"John", "surname":"Doe"] as
Dictionary<String, String>
let jsonData = try? JSONSerialization.data(withJSONObject:
json)
```

Set our custom request headers.

```
req.httpMethod = "POST"
req.httpBody   = jsonData

req.addValue("application/json", forHTTPHeaderField: "Content-
Type")
req.addValue("application/json", forHTTPHeaderField: "Accept")
```

Then, we either create a new "session", or use `URLSession.shared`

Note   URLSession.shared is not yet implemented for Linux

```
let session = URLSession(configuration:
URLSessionConfiguration.default)
```

Then, we create the HTTP task.

```
let task = session.dataTask(with: req) { data, response, error
in

    if error != nil {
        print("Error: \(error)")
    } else {

        // Everything went fine
        // Let's check out what the response was

        if let response = response {
            print("Response: \(response)")
        }

        // And we can also check if there's data for us

        if let data = data,
           let dataStr = String(data: data, encoding:
           .utf8) {

            // And print the data string too

            print ("Data: \(dataStr)")

        }

    }
}
```

Here, we actually execute the task.

Note   If you forget this step, the task - you created it just fine, yep - but it will never run.

```
task.resume()
```

We have to add some delay here. Otherwise, the app will quit before the server sends a response.

```
sleep(5)
```

How It Works

In order to make an HTTP GET request, we may use the URLRequest and URLSession classes, which will help us create an asynchronous task along with its callback.

```
Response: <NSHTTPURLResponse: 0x7fb8f7943a20> { URL: http://
insili.co.uk/iswift/post_json.php } { status code: 200, headers
{
    Connection = "keep-alive";
    "Content-Encoding" = gzip;
    "Content-Type" = "text/html";
    Date = "Sat, 11 Mar 2017 11:39:22 GMT";
    Server = "nginx/1.10.3";
    "Transfer-Encoding" = Identity;
} }
Data: <h1>Json POST request received.</h1>
Array
(
    [name] => John
    [surname] => Doe
)
```

12-32. Make an HTTP POST request

Problem

I want to make an HTTP POST request.

Solution

```
import Foundation
```

First, we create our URL request.

```
let url = URL(string: "http://insili.co.uk/iswift/post.php")
var req = URLRequest(url: url!)
```

Set our request data.

```
req.httpMethod = "POST"
req.httpBody    = "a=someStr&b=anotherVal&c=15".data(using:
.utf8)
```

Then, we either create a new "session", or use URLSession.shared

---

Note URLSession.shared is not yet implemented for Linux

```
let session = URLSession(configuration:
URLSessionConfiguration.default)
```

Then, we create the HTTP task.

```
let task = session.dataTask(with: req) { data, response, error
in

    if error != nil {
        print("Error: \(error)")
    } else {
```

```
        // Everything went fine
        // Let's check out what the response was

        if let response = response {
            print("Response: \(response)")
        }

        // And we can also check if there's data for us

        if let data = data,
           let dataStr = String(data: data, encoding:
           .utf8) {

               // And print the data string too

               print ("Data: \(dataStr)")

        }

    }
}
```

Here, we actually execute the task.

Note   If you forget this step, the task - you created it just fine, yep - but it will never run.

```
task.resume()
```

We have to add some delay here. Otherwise, the app will quit before the server sends a response.

```
sleep(5)
```

How It Works

In order to make an *HTTP POST request*, we may use the URLRequest and URLSession classes, which will help us create an asynchronous task along with its callback.

```
Response: <NSHTTPURLResponse: 0x7fce005d7070> { URL: http://
insili.co.uk/iswift/post.php } { status code: 200, headers {
    Connection = "keep-alive";
    "Content-Encoding" = gzip;
    "Content-Type" = "text/html";
    Date = "Sat, 11 Mar 2017 11:39:12 GMT";
    Server = "nginx/1.10.3";
    "Transfer-Encoding" = Identity;
} }
Data: <h1>POST request received.</h1>
Array
(
    [a] => someStr
    [b] => anotherVal
    [c] => 15
)
```

12-33. Extract components from URL

Problem

I want to get the different components of a specific URL.

Solution

```
import Foundation
```

First, we set our test URL.

```
let url = "http://mydomain.com/test/blog/index.
php?q=1&show=true"
```

Then, we extract the components.

```
if let components = URLComponents(string: url) {

    // Let's retrieve them one by one

    let scheme  = components.scheme
    let host    = components.host
    let path    = components.path
    let query   = components.query

    // And print them out
    // Note: .scheme, .host, and .query return optionals,
    // but in this particular case, it's rather safe to
        force-unwrap them

    print("Scheme: \(scheme!)")
    print("Host: \(host!)")
    print("Path: \(path)")
    print("Query: \(query!)")
}
```

How It Works

In order to extract the different components of a given URL, we may use the URLComponents class.

```
Scheme: http
Host: mydomain.com
Path: /test/blog/index.php
Query: q=1&show=true
```

12-34. Get bundle identifier

Problem

I want to get the identifier of a specific bundle.

Solution

```
import Foundation
```

First, let's get our identifier.

```
if let id = Bundle.main.bundleIdentifier {

    // And print it out

    print("Bundle Identifier: \(id)")
} else {

    print("Error getting bundle identifier.")

}
```

How It Works

In order to get our app bundle's identifier, we may use Bundle's bundleIdentifier property.

```
Error getting bundle identifier.
```

12-35. Get command line arguments

Problem

I want to be able to process the individual command line arguments passed to my application.

Solution

App has just started - what about storing our arguments.

```
let args = CommandLine.arguments
```

Let's see what we have here.

Note   The first item in the array will always be the name of the script itself.

```
print("Command line arguments: \(args)")
```

How It Works

If you have a console application and want to access the command line arguments, that can be easily achieved via CommandLine's `arguments` property.

```
Command line arguments: ["tmp.swift"]
```

12-36. Get executable path from bundle

Problem

I want to get the executables' path of a specific bundle.

Solution

```
import Foundation
```

Let's get our executables' path.

```
if let path = Bundle.main.executablePath {

    // Print it out

    print("Path: \(path)")
} else {

    print("Error getting path for executables.")
}
```

How It Works

In order to get the full path for the executables` folder in our app bundle, we may use Bundle's executablePath property.

```
Path: /Applications/Xcode.app/Contents/Developer/Toolchains/
XcodeDefault.xctoolchain/usr/bin/swift
```

12-37. Get frameworks path from bundle

Problem

I want to get the frameworks' path of a specific bundle.

Solution

```
import Foundation
```

First, let's get our private frameworks' paths.

```
if let privatePath = Bundle.main.privateFrameworksPath {

    // Print it out
```

```
    print("Private Frameworks: \(privatePath)")

} else {

    print("Error getting path for private frameworks.")
}
```

Then, let's get our shared frameworks' paths.

```
if let sharedPath = Bundle.main.sharedFrameworksPath {

    // Print it out

    print("Shared Frameworks: \(sharedPath)")

} else {

    print("Error getting path for shared frameworks.")
}
```

How It Works

In order to get the full path for the frameworks folder in our app bundle, we may use Bundle's sharedFrameworksPath and privateFrameworksPath properties.

```
Private Frameworks: /Applications/Xcode.app/Contents/Developer/
Toolchains/XcodeDefault.xctoolchain/usr/bin/Frameworks
Shared Frameworks: /Applications/Xcode.app/Contents/Developer/
Toolchains/XcodeDefault.xctoolchain/usr/bin/SharedFrameworks
```

12-38. Get home directory for current user
Problem

I want to get the Home directory path for the current user.

Solution

```
import Foundation
```

Get the user's home directory.

```
let home = NSHomeDirectory()
```

And print it out...

```
print("Home: \(home)")
```

How It Works

In order to get the current user's home folder, we may use the NSHomeDirectory function.

```
Home: /Users/drkameleon
```

12-39. Get home directory for user

Problem

I want to get the Home directory path for a specific user.

Solution

```
import Foundation
```

Get the user's home directory

```
if let home = NSHomeDirectoryForUser("user") {
    // And print it out
    print("Home: \(home)")
} else {
    print("Ooops: User not found.")
}
```

How It Works

In order to get the home folder of a given user, we may use the
`NSHomeDirectoryForUser` function.

```
Ooops: User not found.
```

12-40. Get main path for bundle
Problem

I want to get the main path of a given bundle.

Solution

```
import Foundation
```

First, let's get our path.

```
let path = Bundle.main.bundlePath
```

And print it out...

```
print("Path: \(path)")
```

How It Works

In order to get the full path of our app bundle, we may use Bundle's
bundlePath property.

```
Path: /Applications/Xcode.app/Contents/Developer/Toolchains/
XcodeDefault.xctoolchain/usr/bin
```

12-41. Get system currency code

Problem

I want to get the system's default currency code.

Solution

```
import Foundation
```

First, we initialize our Locale object.

```
let locale = Locale.current
```

Extract the currency code.

```
if let currency = locale.currencyCode {

    // And print it out

    print("Currency: \(currency)")

} else {
    print("System currency not set.")
}
```

How It Works

In order to get the system currency code, you may use the Locale class.

```
Currency: USD
```

12-42. Get system language code

Problem

I want to get the system's default language code.

Solution

```
import Foundation
```

First, we initialize our Locale object.

```
let locale = Locale.current
```

Extract the language code.

```
if let language = locale.languageCode {
    // And print it out
    print("Language: \(language)")
} else {
    print("System language not set.")
}
```

How It Works

In order to get the system language code, you may use the Locale class.

```
Language: en
```

12-43. Get system region code

Problem

I want to get the system's default region code.

Solution

```
import Foundation
```

First, we initialize our `Locale` object.

```
let locale = Locale.current
```

Extract the region code.

```
if let region = locale.regionCode {

    // And print it out

    print("Region: \(region)")

} else {
    print("System region not set.")
}
```

How It Works

In order to get the system region code, you may use the `Locale` class.

```
Region: US
```

12-44. Get system temporary directory

Problem

I want to get the system's default temporary directory path.

Solution

```
import Foundation
```

Get the temporary directory.

```
let temp = NSTemporaryDirectory()
```

And print it out...

```
print("Temp: \(temp)")
```

How It Works

In order to get the system's temporary folder path, we may use the NSTemporaryDirectory function.

```
Temp: /var/folders/g1/0j8w3xss4w97cn076v9dwhyr0000gn/T/
```

12-45. Get username of current user
Problem

I want to get the username of the current user.

Solution

```
import Foundation
```

Get the user's username.

```
let username = NSUserName()
```

And print it out...

```
print("Username: \(username)")
```

How It Works

In order to get the current user's username, we may use the NSUserName function.

```
Username: drkameleon
```

12-46. Read input from command line

Problem

I want to be able to get user input from the command line.

Solution

Let's print some welcome message.

```
print("Welcome! Please enter your name:")

if let name = readLine() {

    // And greet our user

    print("Hello, \(name)!")

}
```

How It Works

If you have a console application and want to read user input from the keyboard, that can be easily achieved by using the readLine function, which can be easily achieved via CommandLine's arguments property.

12-47. Summary

In this chapter, we learned how we can make the most out of Swift when dealing with Files, the Web, as well as various more... low-level system functions.

In the next – and last - one, we'll be looking more deeply at some more advanced techniques, mainly working with tasks and processes.

CHAPTER 13

More Advanced Topics

An application usually deals with things in a sequential way, more like a regular cooking recipe: 1, 2, 3, etc.

In this chapter, we'll see how we can break this circle and interact with the system in a more natural way, either by executing commands in the terminal (pretty much as a normal user would) or launch asynchronous processes, which do what they have to in the background but still maintain contact with our main application.

13-1. Execute terminal command
Problem

I want to execute some terminal command and get the result.

Solution

```
import Foundation
```

First, we create our Process and Pipe instances.

Note   On Linux, Process is called Task.

© Yanis Zafirópulos 2019
Y. Zafirópulos, *Swift 4 Recipes*, https://doi.org/10.1007/978-1-4842-4182-0_13

```
let process = Process()
let pipe = Pipe()
```

Set our process's details, basically: which specific command we are going to run and with what arguments.

```
process.launchPath = "/usr/bin/env"
process.arguments = ["pwd"]
```

Connect the pipe to our process, so that we can receive its output.

```
process.standardOutput = pipe
```

And fire it up! :)

```
process.launch()
process.waitUntilExit()
```

After it finishes, it's time to retrieve the result.

```
let data = pipe.fileHandleForReading.readDataToEndOfFile()

if let result = String(data: data, encoding: .utf8) {

    // Finally, let's print it out

    print("pwd => \(result)")

}
```

How It Works

In order to run a shell command or subscript, we may make use of the very handy Process and Pipe classes.

```
pwd => /tests/swift/v4
```

13-2. Execute terminal command asynchronously

Problem

I want to execute a terminal command in an asynchronous way and get the result.

Solution

```
import Foundation
import Dispatch
```

Let's make sure we're on OSX 10.10 or newer. Otherwise, this won't work.

```
if #available(OSX 10.10, *) {

    // First we create our Process and Pipe instances
    // Note: On Linux, Process is called Task

    let process = Process()
    let pipe = Pipe()

    // Here, we wrap up all of the 'async' part

    DispatchQueue.global().async {

        // Set our process's details
        // basically: which specific command we are going
        //     to run
        // and with what arguments

        process.launchPath = "/usr/bin/env"
        process.arguments = ["pwd"]
```

```swift
            // Connect the pipe to our process,
            // so that we can receive its output

            process.standardOutput = pipe

            // And fire it up! :)

            process.launch()
            process.waitUntilExit()

            // After it finishes,
            // it's time to retrieve the result

            let data = pipe.fileHandleForReading.
            readDataToEndOfFile()

            if let result = String(data: data, encoding: .utf8)
{

                // Finally, let's print it out

                print("pwd => \(result)")

            }

        }

        // Print something out - synchronously

        print("Just launched the task")

        // Create a delay of 2 seconds,
        // to give it some time to perform all async actions

        sleep(2)

} else {
        print(":-(")
}
```

How It Works

In order to run a shell command or subscript, we may make use of the very handy `Process` and `Pipe` classes.

```
Just launched the task
pwd => /tests/swift/v4
```

13-3. Execute asynchronous task

Problem

I want to execute a task, in an asynchronous way.

Solution

```
import Dispatch
import Foundation
```

Let's start.

```
print("Starting out...")
```

Let's make sure we're on OSX 10.10 or newer.
Otherwise, this won't work.

```
if #available(OSX 10.10, *) {

    // This is an asynchronous task

    DispatchQueue.global().async {

        print("Task A: Believe or not, I'm asynchronous")

        for i in 0..<5 {
            print("Task A: Counting \(i)")
```

```
        }
    }

    // This is another asynchronous task

    DispatchQueue.global().async {

        print("Task B: I'm asynchronous as well")

        for i in 0..<5 {
            print("Task B: Counting \(i)")
        }
    }

    // Let's print something to make sure where we are
    // synchronously this time

    print("Just launched all tasks!")

    // Create a delay of 2 seconds,
    // to give it some time to perform all async actions

    sleep(2)
} else {
    print(":-(")
}
```

How It Works

In order to execute an asynchronous task, we may use DispatchQueue's async method and then wrap up all of our asynchronous statements.

```
Starting out...
Just launched all tasks!
Task A: Believe or not, I'm asynchronous
```

```
Task B: I'm asynchronous as well
Task A: Counting 0
Task B: Counting 0
Task A: Counting 1
Task B: Counting 1
Task A: Counting 2
Task B: Counting 2
Task A: Counting 3
Task B: Counting 3
Task A: Counting 4
Task B: Counting 4
```

13-4. Create a delay

Problem

I want to create some specific delay.

Solution

```
import Foundation
```

Let's print something to get started.

```
print("Hello world - I'm about to delay a bit...")
```

Create a delay of 2 seconds.

```
sleep(2)
```

And return...

```
print("Hey, I'm back! :)")
```

How It Works

In order to create a delay of some seconds, in the current thread, we may use the sleep function.

```
Hello world - I'm about to delay a bit...
Hey, I'm back! :)
```

13-5. Defer execution of code

Problem

I want to defer the execute of a specific block of code.

Solution

Let's create an example function.

```
func doSomething() {
     print("doSomething: Here we are!")

     defer {
           // This is our deferred block.
           // This is going to be execute just before leaving
               the function

           print("doSomething: Just leaving the function")
     }
     // Let's do something... finally!

     for i in 0...10 {
           print("doSomething: i = \(i)").
     }
}
print("Before calling our function...")
```

356

Let's call our function.

```
doSomething()
```

And let's print something, so that we know we are back.

```
print("After calling our function")
```

How It Works

In order to defer code execution, that is: to delay the execution of a given block of code, until the app exits current scope (e.g., function), mainly for "housekeeping," like closing an open connection, or an open file, etc., we can use the defer keyword followed by our *deferred* code block.

```
Before calling our function...
doSomething: Here we are!
doSomething: i = 0
doSomething: i = 1
doSomething: i = 2
doSomething: i = 3
doSomething: i = 4
doSomething: i = 5
doSomething: i = 6
doSomething: i = 7
doSomething: i = 8
doSomething: i = 9
doSomething: i = 10
doSomething: Just leaving the function
After calling our function.
```

13-6. Get type of variable

Problem

I want to get the type of a specific variable..

Solution

Note   The `Mirror` class is not yet available on Linux.

Let's set some variables.

```
let str = "This is a string"
let arr = [1,2,3]
let num = 6
```

Then, we "extract" the types.

```
let strType = Mirror(reflecting: str).subjectType
let arrType = Mirror(reflecting: arr).subjectType
let numType = Mirror(reflecting: num).subjectType
```

And, finally, print them out...

```
print("str => \(strType)")
print("arr => \(arrType)")
print("num => \(numType)")
```

How It Works

In order to retrieve the type of a given variable or expression, we may use the very handy `Mirror` class.

```
str => String
arr => Array<Int>
num => Int
```

13-7. Observe variable value changes

Problem

I want to be able to observe the value changes of a specific variable.

Solution

Let's set a variable with some initial value and the appropriate observers.

Note   Inside our "observers," we can always access the `oldValue`, as well as the `newValue`.

```
var temperature = 20 {

    willSet {
        print("Temperature is about to change to
        \(newValue). Get dressed!")
    }

    didSet {
        print("Hmm... Temperature just changed from
        \(oldValue) to \(temperature).")
    }
}
```

Let's change our variable, so that our observers fire up.

```
temperature = 0
```

How It Works

In order to "observe" a value or property for change, that is: to have it notify us whenever it is about to change, or when it has just changed, we may use the `willSet` and `didSet` observers, respectively.

```
Temperature is about to change to 0. Get dressed!
Hmm... Temperature just changed from 20 to 0.
```

13-8. Cache data with NSCache

Problem

I want to cache some data.

Solution

```
import Foundation
```

First, we specify what type of Cache we need.

Let's say an `<NSString,NSString>` Cache, that is: a Cache of `NSString`'s (the first value is our Cache's keys, which will be strings anyway).

Note   Normally, it'd be wiser to have a cache with some really "heavy" objects, and not just string – but whatever... this is just an example, right?

```
var cache = NSCache<NSString,NSString>()
```

Then, we set a couple of objects in our cache.

```
cache.setObject(NSString(string: "one cached object"), forKey:
"one" as NSString)
cache.setObject(NSString(string: "another cached object"),
forKey: "two" as NSString)
```

Now let's try accessing it, as we'd normally do in a real-world application.

```
if let cached = cache.object(forKey: "one") {

    // Yep, we find a cached version for "one",
    // Let's print it out

    print("Found: \(cached)")
} else {

    // Not found? Really?!

    print("In a multi-threaded environment, it's not that
    safe to assume that NSCache returns the object you just
    added. So, don't panic!")
}
```

How It Works

Caching data – especially resource-expensive data – is a great way of speeding up your application. This can be easily achieved using the NSCache class.

```
Found: one cached object
```

13-9. Summary

In this chapter, we covered various advanced programming topics: from executing a simple terminal command, to launching asynchronous tasks/processes, checking the type of a given variable – at execution time – key/value observing, and even being able to cache our data.

Index

Symbols

+ operator, 95, 139
+= operator, 132
== comparison operator, 93,
        136–137, 193, 271
< and > comparison operators, 94

A

acos function, 236
arc4random function, 178
Array
    append method
        existing array, 131–132
        item, 132–133
    capacity, 153
    concatenation, 139
    convert JSON string to
        array, 142–143
    count property, 230
    dictionary's values
        property, 151–152
    element, 133
    empty property, 134
    enumerated method, 139–140
    equal, 135–136

filter method, 149–150, 174
filter element, by index, 173
first element, 154–155
index element, 150–151
index element by value, 154
index/indices of item, 156–158
initializer, 145
insert method, 164, 165, 170–171
join separator method, 165–166
to JSON string, 141–142
last element, 158–159
last X elements, 159–160
with literal, 146
loop, 168
map method, 169
maximum value, 160
minimum value, 161
NSArray object, 147–148
object type, 134–135
random element, 161–162
range creation, 144–145
reduce method, 171–172, 230,
        232–233, 240
removal
    array item by value, 174
    duplicate elements, 174–175